The
Magic In
Metaphor

The Magic In Metaphor

Empowering Children Through Healing Stories

Harley Sears

For Britt and Archie

Contents

Self-Care for Parents, Teachers, Counselors,
and Childcare Providers

About The Author

Introduction

This book is a collection of healing stories designed to support children's emotional and social development and address common behavioral challenges. It is a resource for parents, teachers, counselors, and childcare providers who seek to empower children with the skills and understanding necessary to navigate the complexities of childhood.

Each story in this book is crafted with a therapeutic metaphor, enabling children to relate to the characters and situations while gaining insights into their own experiences. This book covers common childhood challenges, including emotional regulation, self-esteem, anxiety, friendship, empathy, resilience, and more. It also addresses contemporary concerns such as digital safety and environmental awareness.

Metaphors are a powerful tool in storytelling for children because they simplify complex ideas, create emotional connections, encourage imagination, and have universal appeal. By using metaphors, storytellers can create engaging and meaningful narratives that effectively convey important lessons and support the emotional and social development of children.

In addition to captivating narratives, this book offers an extra dimension of guidance through comprehensive analyses that follow each story. By dissecting the key themes and takeaways, "The Magic In Metaphor" is a valuable tool for those seeking to facilitate impactful conversations and promote a deeper understanding of the stories' lessons.

These sections not only delve into the lessons and therapeutic aspects of each tale but also provide clear explanations of the core concepts and messages, making it simple for readers to understand and apply the insights in their own lives or when caring for children. Furthermore, these segments feature suggested activities and a highlight activity, allowing adults to engage in meaningful discussions and foster emotional growth and development in children.

Written in an engaging and accessible style, these stories entertain and provide practical guidance and support for children and adults alike. By addressing everyday challenges and offering actionable strategies, this book fosters emotional well-being, personal growth, and the development of essential life skills.

1

Archie's Doggie Daycare Adventure

Overcoming fear and anxiety, separation anxiety, the power of friendship, emotional expression, resilience and personal growth

In the charming town of Snugglewood, with its cobblestone streets lined with flowering trees, a lovable puppy named Archie stole the hearts of all who met him. Archie spent his days playing with his favorite squeaky toys, running through the park, and snuggling up with his loving family.

One bright and cheerful morning, Archie's family shared an exciting surprise. They were taking him to a wondrous place called "Doggie Daycare." They promised he would meet many new friends and embark on exciting adventures. Although Archie was thrilled, he couldn't shake the butterflies in his tummy. He had never been away from home before and didn't know what to expect.

As they approached Doggie Daycare, Archie's heart fluttered with anticipation. He gazed around and saw puppies of all shapes, sizes, and breeds playing and laughing. However, Archie still felt a little uneasy.

The kind-hearted daycare owner, Miss Mary, noticed Archie's nervousness and gently knelt beside him. She tenderly stroked his fur and whispered: "Archie, even the bravest puppies feel nervous when trying something new. But I assure you, there's nothing to fear here. You're safe and will make many new friends by the end of the day."

Archie's eyes sparkled with wonder as he listened to Miss Mary's comforting words. She introduced him to a lovable dog named Junah, with the most delicate golden fur. Junah was a gentle and patient soul who guided Archie around Doggie Daycare, showing him all the amazing things they could do together. They explored an enchanted play area with a maze of tunnels, a bouncy castle, and a magical pool filled with colorful balls.

As they frolicked and played, Archie learned that Junah had also felt nervous on her first day at Doggie Daycare. Junah explained that her fear faded as she found comfort in the love and support of her new friends. Archie felt his heart swell with warmth and gratitude, knowing he wasn't alone in his feelings.

Throughout the day, Archie made many new friends, each with unique stories of feeling nervous when they first arrived. Yet, they all reassured Archie that he would soon feel right at home. Archie felt a deep sense of belonging and realized that Doggie Daycare was a magical and safe place for everyone.

When it was time for Archie's family to pick him up, his emotions swirled. He was overjoyed to see them but felt a twinge of sadness at leaving his new friends. Archie excitedly recounted his incredible day, and his family beamed with pride, knowing their little puppy had bravely faced his fears and grown even more resilient.

From that day forward, Archie eagerly anticipated each visit to Doggie Daycare. He made lifelong friendships, embarked on fun adventures, and discovered that trying new things could be scary, yet exciting at the same time. Most importantly, Archie learned that with love, encouragement, and the support of his friends, there was nothing he couldn't overcome.

And so, the little puppy named Archie became a symbol of bravery for all young dogs facing their fears and embracing new experiences. His heartwarming tale was a reminder that even when you feel small and vulnerable, the power of love and friendship can help you find the strength to soar above any challenge.

Lessons Revealed

Healing metaphor: This story of Archie's Doggie Daycare Adventure serves as a metaphor for overcoming fears and embracing new experiences. Archie's journey from feeling nervous and uncertain to finding comfort and friendship symbolizes the process of personal growth and development that people of all ages go through when faced with new situations.

Overcoming fear: The story shows how Archie faces his fear of trying something new and unfamiliar. This teaches children that it is normal to feel nervous or scared when facing new situations, but it's important to face those fears and try new experiences.

The power of friendship: Archie's experience demonstrates the importance of friendship and support. Children can learn that making friends and helping one another can ease their fears and make challenging situations more enjoyable.

Emotional expression: The story encourages children to express their feelings and talk about their fears and concerns with others. By sharing their emotions, children can better understand their feelings and seek guidance from those around them.

Resilience and personal growth: Archie's story teaches children that overcoming fears and embracing new experiences can lead to personal growth and resilience. Children can learn that facing challenges head-on can help them develop essential life skills and build their self-confidence.

Empathy and understanding: By hearing about Archie's fears, children can develop empathy and understanding for others who may be going through similar experiences. This can foster a sense of compassion and encourage children to support one another.

Suggested Activities

My first time: Encourage children to write or draw about a time when they faced a new experience or challenge, describing how they felt and overcame their fears.

Role-play: Create role-playing scenarios where children take turns acting as Archie, Junah, and other characters from the story, exploring different situations where they may need to rely on friendship and courage to overcome fears.

Discussion questions: Develop a set of discussion questions that encourage children to think about the story's themes and messages. Discuss how Archie's experience at Doggie Daycare helped him grow and how his new friendships supported him.

The friendship chain: Have children cut and decorate paper strips, writing a friend's name on each strip. Connect the strips to form a chain, symbolizing the support system that friends provide in overcoming fears.

Bravery badges: Invite children to create their own "bravery badges" to wear or display, recognizing their achievements in facing fears and embracing new experiences.

Courage collage: Encourage children to create a collage of images, words, and symbols representing courage and overcoming fears. This visual representation can serve as a reminder of their personal strength.

Coping strategies: Discuss various coping strategies for dealing with fear and anxiety, such as deep breathing, visualization, or positive self-talk. Have children practice these techniques and reflect on which ones work best.

The support team: Have children identify and list the people in their lives who offer support and encouragement when they face challenges or new experiences. Encourage them to share their gratitude with these individuals.

New adventures journal: Provide a journal for children to document their new experiences and associated feelings. Encourage regular entries, reflecting on personal growth and the role of friendship in overcoming fears.

Story extension: Invite children to write or draw a continuation of Archie's adventures, focusing on how he and his friends support each other in facing new challenges and experiences.

"Discussion" Activity

1. How did Archie feel when he first arrived at the doggie daycare? Why do you think he felt that way?

2. What are some ways the dogs at the daycare showed kindness and friendship towards Archie?

3. How did Archie's feelings change as he spent more time at the doggie daycare? What do you think contributed to this change?

4. Can you think of a time when you felt nervous or scared in a new situation? How did you overcome your fears or worries?

5. How do you think the other dogs at the daycare learned to be so kind and understanding toward one another?

6. In the story, Archie learned that each dog at the daycare had unique qualities and talents. Why is it important to recognize and appreciate the differences in others?

7. What are some ways you can show kindness and friendship to others in your daily life?

8. How do you think Archie's experience at the doggie daycare will impact his future interactions with other dogs and new situations?

9. What is the most important lesson you learned from Archie's Doggie Daycare Adventure?

2

The Worry Web

Addressing anxiety and worry, importance of communication, empathy and support, the power of friendship, hope and positivity

Once upon a time, a little ladybug named Lyla lived in an enchanting garden filled with vibrant flowers and delightful creatures. Lyla's glossy red wings were adorned with jet-black spots, and she was renowned for her compassionate heart and cheerful spirit.

One morning, as the first light of dawn kissed the dewdrops on the petals, Lyla awoke to the musical sounds of her garden friends.

With a flutter of her wings, she eagerly prepared for another day of wondrous exploration. But as she soared towards the petals of her favorite flower, she noticed something strange.

In the heart of the garden, where the most glorious flowers once blossomed and the air buzzed with energy, stood a vast dark web. This was the Worry Web, and with every moment that passed, it grew deep and wide. Unlike the glistening creations of her spider friends, this web was a dark, twisted mass that seemed to cast a heavy shadow over the otherwise joyful garden.

Intrigued and concerned, Lyla bravely approached the web. As she drew closer, she discovered that her fellow garden friends were trapped in its tangled threads. The once vibrant butterflies, bees, and dragonfly's appeared listless and subdued, their colors muted by the Worry Web's suffocating grasp.

Determined to rescue her friends, Lyla inhaled deeply and fluttered her wings with renewed purpose. She gently encouraged each creature to share their anxieties and fears. As they spoke, Lyla listened carefully and offered soothing words of comfort and reassurance. The Worry Web's grip weakened with each concern shared, and the garden's natural splendor slowly re-emerged.

One by one, the garden dwellers broke free from the Worry Web's clutches, their laughter and friendship filling the air once more. The web, now diminished by the power of love and understanding, retreated and evaporated into thin air.

Lyla realized that the Worry Web had been a powerful symbol for the stress and anxiety that can consume us if we don't confront our fears and seek solace in the love and support of those around us. As the final thread of worry faded, the garden evolved into the Magical Garden of Serenity. The once ordinary flowers now shimmered with rainbow colors, and a gentle, soothing breeze carried the sweet scent of lavender.

From that day forward, Lyla and her garden friends vowed to share their worries and support each other through thick and thin. The Magical Garden of Serenity thrived, and they all lived happily ever after, confident that together, they could overcome any Worry Web that threatened to trap their magnificent world.

And so, Lyla the Ladybug taught the inhabitants of the Magical Garden of Serenity, and all who heard her tale, that when we open our hearts and lean on one another, even the most threatening web of worry can be conquered, transforming our world into a place of love, understanding, and serenity.

Lessons Revealed

Healing metaphor: The Worry Web symbolizes the stress, anxiety, and fear that can consume individuals when they don't address their concerns or seek support from others. The Magical Garden of Serenity represents a harmonious state achieved through open communication, empathy, and understanding.

Addressing anxiety and worry: The story highlights the Worry Web as a symbol of stress and anxiety, teaching children that everyone sometimes experiences these feelings. It encourages them to acknowledge and confront their fears rather than letting them grow and consume them.

Importance of communication: Lyla encourages the garden creatures to share their anxieties and fears, demonstrating the importance of open communication. Children can learn that talking about their worries with others can help alleviate stress and make them feel better.

Empathy and support: The story shows how Lyla listens carefully to her friends' concerns and offers comforting words. This can teach children the value of empathy and the significance of providing emotional support to their friends and loved ones.

The power of friendship: Lyla and the garden creatures overcome the Worry Web together, emphasizing the importance of friendship and teamwork. Children can learn that leaning on one another and offering support can help them overcome challenges and foster a sense of belonging.

Hope and positivity: The transformation of the garden into the Magical Garden of Serenity shows that positive outcomes are possible when individuals face their worries and support each other.

Suggested Activities

Drawing: Encourage children to draw their own Worry Web, illustrating the worries they feel are trapping them. Discuss ways to untangle each concern and free themselves from the web.

Sharing circle: Create a safe space for children to share their concerns and anxieties, reinforcing the importance of talking about their feelings and supporting one another.

Coping skills toolbox: Have children brainstorm and list healthy coping strategies for dealing with anxiety and stress. They can create a personalized "toolbox" containing these strategies, which they can use when faced with challenges.

Problem-solving scenarios: Present children with hypothetical situations in which a character is trapped in a Worry Web. Encourage them to come up with solutions to overcome their worries.

Role-play: Have children role-play as Lyla and her garden friends, acting out scenes from the story that emphasizes the importance of empathy, understanding, and communication in overcoming anxiety.

Worry stones: Provide children with smooth stones to decorate and keep as "worry stones." They can hold these stones when they feel anxious as a reminder to share their worries and seek support.

Positive affirmations: Encourage children to create a list of positive affirmations to recite when they feel trapped in their Worry Web. Affirmations can help boost self-esteem and empower children to overcome their anxieties.

Gratitude garden: Have children create a "gratitude garden" by drawing or writing things they are grateful for on colorful paper flowers. Display the flowers in a prominent place as a reminder of the positive aspects of their lives.

Mindfulness and relaxation techniques: Teach children various mindfulness and relaxation techniques, such as deep breathing, progressive muscle relaxation, and guided imagery, to help them manage their stress and anxiety.

Story extension: Invite children to write or draw their own continuation of Lyla's adventures in the Magical Garden of Serenity, focusing on how she and her friends continue to support each other in facing their worries and challenges.

"Worry Stones" Activity

Materials:

- Smooth, flat stones or pebbles (1-2 inches in diameter)
- Acrylic paint or paint pens (in various colors)
- Paintbrushes (if using acrylic paint)
- A small cup of water (to rinse brushes)
- A palette or a disposable plate (for mixing paint colors)
- Clear sealant spray or Mod Podge (for sealing the paint)
- Paper towels or cloth (for cleaning up any spills or messes)
- Newspapers or drop cloth (to protect your work surfaces)

Instructions:

1. Prepare your work area by covering it with newspapers or a drop cloth to protect the surface from paint spills.

2. Choose a smooth, flat stone or pebble that fits comfortably in your hand. Make sure it's clean and dry before you begin painting.

3. Using acrylic paint or paint pens, decorate your worry stone with colors, patterns, or words that make you feel calm and relaxed. You can paint a simple design or write an inspirational word or phrase.

4. Allow the paint to dry completely. This may take a few hours, depending on the thickness of the paint.

5. If you'd like to seal the paint on your worry stone, apply a coat of clear sealant spray or Mod Podge. This will help protect the paint from chipping or fading. Allow the sealant to dry according to the manufacturer's instructions.

6. Once your worry stone is dry, hold it in your hand and gently rub your thumb or fingers over the smooth surface. Use the worry stone to help you focus on positive thoughts and feelings when feeling anxious or stressed.

7. Keep your worry stone in your pocket or bag so it's always available when needed. You can also create multiple worry stones with different designs or words to use in various situations or to share with friends and family members who benefit from their calming effects.

3

Flicker's Fearless Night

Facing fears, fear of the dark, inner strength, the power of wisdom and guidance, appreciating differences, finding beauty in the unknown

In a peaceful meadow where wildflowers danced in the gentle breeze, and the tall grasses rustled with the chirping of crickets, there lived a young and curious firefly named Flicker.

Flicker dazzled all the creatures around him with his brilliant glow, which twinkled like a bright starry night. Despite this, Flicker found himself gripped by fear when the daylight faded and the darkness of night crept in.

One warm summer evening, Flicker's wise old friend, Grandfather Owl, called out to the little firefly from the highest branch of an old oak tree. "Flicker, my dear," he said in his deep, calming voice, "I have a magical story to share with you, a tale of courage and light that I believe will help you overcome your fear and embrace the beauty of the night."

Flicker buzzed up to the branch near Grandfather Owl's kind old face, his wings shimmering with excitement. He nestled close, ready to listen. The wise owl began sharing the enchanting story of the Sun and the Moon, two eternal companions who ruled the sky, each with their own special light and purpose.

"The Sun," Grandfather Owl began, his eyes twinkling with wisdom, "shines brightly during the day, spreading warmth and light all over the land. He brings happiness and energy to every living being, helping them to grow and flourish. But when the Sun needs to rest, his dear friend, the Moon, takes over."

"The Moon," he continued, "watches over the night with her silvery, soothing light. She casts a gentle glow that guides the nighttime creatures and comforts the restless ones. Although her light is not as bright as the Sun's, it's just as important because it helps the world find rest, peace, and balance."

Flicker listened carefully, captivated by the mesmerizing story of these two cosmic friends. As the tale unraveled, Grandfather Owl described how the Moon's silver glow helped the forest animals find their path in the darkness, bringing a sense of calm and safety. The Moon's gentle light was a guiding star and a symbol of protection.

"Flicker," Grandfather Owl whispered gently, "you are like the Moon in your special way. Your light may be small, but it is powerful and can guide others through the darkness. Embrace your inner light, and never fear the night again."

As Flicker pondered Grandfather Owl's words, he understood that he had focused on the darkness rather than the light within himself. From then on, whenever Flicker was afraid, he would recall the magical story of the Sun and the Moon and the strength of his inner light.

Gradually, Flicker started to appreciate the beauty of the night, realizing it was an opportunity to share his light with the world. As he glowed brighter and brighter, others took notice, and they, too, began to find comfort in the darkness.

And so, with the help of Grandfather Owl's enchanting tale and the wisdom of the Sun and the Moon, Flicker learned to face his fears and let his light shine, brightening the shadowy corners of the meadow and inspiring others to discover their own inner light.

Lessons Revealed

Healing metaphor: The metaphor in this story lies in Flicker's fear of the darkness and his ability to shine his light, which represents facing one's fears and embracing one's own inner strength and resilience to help guide and inspire others in challenging situations.

Facing fears: Flicker's journey to overcome his fear of the dark illustrates that everyone has fears, and it's essential to confront and face them. Children can learn that working through their fears can lead to personal growth and confidence.

Inner strength: The story teaches children that they have an inner light or strength to help them navigate difficult situations, like Flicker's realization about his glow. This lesson encourages children to believe in themselves and their abilities.

The power of wisdom and guidance: Grandfather Owl's role in the story demonstrates the importance of seeking guidance from wise and trusted individuals. Children can learn the value of listening to the experiences and wisdom of others to help them navigate their own challenges.

Appreciating differences: The tale of the Sun and the Moon emphasizes that different qualities and strengths can be equally valuable. Children can learn to appreciate and embrace their unique qualities and understand that everyone has something special to offer.

Finding beauty in the unknown: Flicker's transformation helps him see the beauty of the night, which he once feared. This can teach children to approach unfamiliar or seemingly scary situations with curiosity and an open mind, seeking out the positive aspects rather than focusing on fear.

Suggested Activities

Inner light collage: Have children create a collage representing their inner light, highlighting their strengths, talents, and what makes them unique. This activity encourages self-awareness and helps children focus on their positive traits.

Fear exploration: Encourage children to identify and discuss their fears and help them brainstorm ways to confront and overcome them. This activity promotes problem-solving and resilience.

Nighttime adventures: Organize a supervised nighttime walk or stargazing activity, allowing children to experience the beauty of the night and learn that it can be a safe and enjoyable time.

Guided visualization: Lead children through a guided visualization where they imagine themselves as Flicker, embracing their inner light and conquering their fears. This activity helps children build self-confidence and develop coping skills.

Sharing circle: Create a safe space for children to share their fears and discuss ways they can help each other overcome them, emphasizing the importance of empathy and teamwork.

Moon and Sun art: Have children create artwork depicting the Sun and the Moon, focusing on their unique qualities and the balance they bring to the world. This activity encourages children to appreciate the importance of balance in their lives.

Story extension: Invite children to write or draw their own continuation of Flicker's story, highlighting how he continues to face his fears and help others in the meadow.

Light and dark activities: Organize activities that explore the concept of light and dark, such as shadow play or creating lanterns. These activities can help children understand the contrast between light and dark and appreciate the beauty of both.

Positive affirmations: Encourage children to create a list of positive affirmations that they can recite when they feel scared or anxious, boosting their self-esteem and empowering them to face their fears.

Gratitude journal: Have children keep a gratitude journal where they write down things they are grateful for each day. Focusing on gratitude can help shift their perspective from fear to appreciation and promote a positive mindset.

"Guided Imagery" Activity

This guided imagery activity will help children imagine themselves in a calming, safe space, similar to Flicker's experience in the story. It can help children relax and feel more at ease when they are anxious or afraid, particularly at night.

Instructions:

1. Find a comfortable and quiet place for the child to sit or lie down. Please make sure they are in a relaxed position and can listen without distractions.

2. Begin the guided visualization by reading the following script slowly and calmly. Encourage the child to close their eyes and focus on the words as you guide them through the visualization.

"Take a deep breath in, and slowly breathe out. Feel your body becoming more and more relaxed.

Now, imagine standing in a beautiful, magical forest at night. The sky above is filled with twinkling stars, and the air is cool and fresh. As you look around, you notice the trees glowing softly with different colors, just like Flicker in the story.

As you walk through the forest, you come across a small, shimmering pond. The water is crystal clear, reflecting the stars and the colors of the glowing trees. The sight is comforting and calming.

You sit by the water, feeling the soft grass beneath you. You notice a group of friendly fireflies glowing with a warm, gentle light. They come closer, dancing around you and creating a magical atmosphere.

Feel the warmth and comfort of the fireflies' light as they surround you, making you feel safe and protected. As you watch their graceful movements, your fears and worries fade away.

Take a moment to enjoy the peacefulness of this magical forest, knowing that you are safe and protected by the gentle light of the fireflies.

When you are ready, take a deep breath and slowly breathe out. Bring your awareness back to the room and gently open your eyes."

3. After the guided imagery, encourage the child to share their experience. You can ask questions like:

- How did it feel to be in the magical forest?
- What colors were the glowing trees?
- How did the fireflies' light make you feel?

4. Remind the child that they can always return to this magical, safe place in their imagination whenever they need to feel calm and secure. Practicing this guided imagery can help children build their inner sense of safety and reduce anxiety or fear they may have during the nighttime.

4

Heckle's Heartfelt Transformation

Bullying, empathy and compassion, personal growth and change,
consequences of actions, power of positive influence

Once upon a time, a young hyena named Heckle lived in the warm, golden savanna. Heckle was notorious for his harsh laugh and a cruel sense of humor. He often roamed the plains, seeking other animals to taunt and tease. The other animals dreaded encountering Heckle, as his hurtful words and mean-spirited pranks cast a dark cloud over their lives.

One fateful day, a new creature arrived on the savanna, a kind and gentle giraffe named Grace. With her warm and compassionate presence, Grace quickly sensed the tension and sorrow among the animals. Intrigued, she asked a young zebra, "Why do all the animals here seem so unhappy?"

The zebra hesitated momentarily before confiding in Grace, "It's because of Heckle the Hyena. His ruthless taunting and teasing have made us all miserable. We're at a loss for how to make him stop."

The news deeply saddened Grace, but she was determined to confront Heckle and help him understand the consequences of his actions. She searched for Heckle and soon found him mocking a turtle for its slow pace.

"Heckle," Grace said firmly but kindly, "are you aware of the pain and suffering your words and actions inflict upon others?" Heckle sneered at Grace and replied arrogantly, "Why should I care? It's just a bit of fun and makes me feel powerful."

Grace gazed at Heckle compassionately and suggested, "True strength and power come from kindness, understanding, and empowering others, not bullying them. I challenge you to change your habits for one week. You can return to your old ways if you don't experience any positive changes."

Heckle was skeptical, but his curiosity grew, and he reluctantly agreed to the challenge.

Over the next week, Heckle tried to change his behavior. At first, he found it challenging to be kind, but as he practiced listening and offered words of support, he gradually noticed a change. The other animals became less nervous around him and even greeted him with smiles and warm hellos.

At the end of the week, Heckle met with Grace, and she asked about his experience. Surprisingly, Heckle realized he felt happier and more connected than ever.

"I never thought I could feel this way," Heckle confessed. "By being kind, I've developed genuine friendships, and I feel truly powerful, not because I'm causing others pain, but because I'm helping them thrive."

Grace beamed at Heckle and explained, "That's the beauty of kindness. When we lift others, we rise with them."

From that day forward, Heckle the Hyena continued on his path of empathy and compassion, and the animals of the savanna discovered a newfound sense of unity and joy.

And so, Heckle transformed not only himself but also the lives of all those who called the savanna their home, proving that even the most hardened hearts can soften over time.

Lessons Revealed

Healing metaphor: The metaphor in this story is Heckle's transformation from cruel and hurtful to kind and compassionate.

This represents the power of personal growth and the ability of anyone to change their behavior and positively impact the lives of others, fostering a sense of unity and happiness within a community.

The importance of empathy and compassion: The story shows how Heckle's transformation positively impacts the savanna community. Children can learn the value of being kind, understanding, and empathetic towards others.

Personal growth and change: Heckle's journey illustrates that everyone has the potential for personal growth and change, even when they seem resistant to it. Children can learn that they are capable of self-improvement and that it's never too late to become a better person.

Consequences of actions: Through the story, children can understand that their words and actions affect others. This can help them develop a greater sense of responsibility and consideration for the feelings of those around them.

The power of positive influence: Grace's gentle guidance helps Heckle see the error of his ways and embrace change. Children can learn that they can positively influence others, and sometimes, all it takes is a little patience, understanding, and support.

Building healthy relationships: As Heckle learns to be kind, he develops genuine friendships with the other animals. This can teach children the importance of treating others with respect and compassion to foster healthy relationships.

Suggested Activities

Kindness challenge: Encourage children to participate in a week-long kindness challenge similar to the one Heckle underwent in the story. Have them perform at least one act of kindness each day and document their experience in the workbook.

Feelings chart: Provide a feelings chart or emotion wheel for children to explore and identify the emotions experienced by the characters in the story. Discuss how each character might have felt and why.

Journal prompts: Create journal prompts that encourage children to reflect on their own experiences with teasing or being teased, how they handled it, and how they could show empathy and kindness to others in similar situations.

Acts of kindness brainstorm: Have children brainstorm a list of kind actions they could perform daily. Encourage them to develop ideas relating to their school, home, and community environments.

Story discussion questions: Create a set of discussion questions that encourage children to think about the story's themes and messages. Discuss how Heckle's transformation affected the other animals and what they learned from his change.

Draw your own story: Invite children to create their own illustrations or comic strips inspired by the story, focusing on key moments of kindness, empathy, and personal growth.

The power of apologies: Discuss the importance of apologizing when we hurt others and provide examples of sincere apologies. Have children practice apologizing through role-playing.

Create a kindness pledge: Encourage children to create their own kindness pledges, outlining specific ways they commit to being more empathetic and compassionate toward others.

Kindness reflection: Have the children reflect on any changes they've noticed in their own feelings, behaviors, and relationships as a result of practicing kindness and empathy.

"Journal" Activity

These journal prompts are designed to encourage children to reflect on their feelings, emotions, and actions, just like Heckle in the story. By completing these prompts, children can develop a better understanding of their emotions and how they can react positively to different situations.

Materials:

- A notebook or journal
- Pen, pencil, or other writing instruments
- Colored pencils, markers, or crayons for drawing or decorating

Journal Prompts:

1. Think about a time when you felt angry or upset. Describe the situation and how it made you feel. What did you do to handle your feelings?

2. What are some positive ways you can express your emotions when angry or frustrated? Make a list of at least three strategies you can use in the future.

3. Heckle learned to turn his negative feelings into positive actions in the story. Can you think of a time when you turned a negative experience into a positive one? Describe what happened and how you were able to transform the situation.

4. Write a letter to yourself about the importance of empathy and understanding. What can you do to understand better and support the feelings of others around you?

5. Imagine that you have a friend struggling with their emotions, just like Heckle. Write a note to your friend, offering them encouragement and advice on dealing with their feelings positively.

6. Reflect on your own emotions and how they change throughout the day. Create a feelings chart or drawing that represents the different emotions you experience and when you typically feel them.

7. Write about a person or pet who has helped you through a challenging time. What did they do to support you, and how did it make you feel?

Encourage children to spend time working on these journal prompts, either individually or as a group activity. Give them ample time to think, write, and draw in their journals. After completing the prompts, children can share their thoughts and experiences with their peers or family members.

5

Buzzy's Blossoming Friendships

*Importance of friendships, patience and resilience, care and respect,
nurturing friendships, appreciating diversity*

In the heart of a vibrant meadow, a bumblebee named Buzzy spent his days darting from flower to flower. Although the meadow was home to many creatures, Buzzy had never ventured far from his nest to make friends with them.

One sunny morning, as Buzzy whizzed around the meadow, he noticed a beautiful garden in the distance. It was unlike anything he had ever seen, with a diverse collection of plants and flowers. Buzzy was curious and decided to take a break from his usual routine to explore the garden.

Buzzy discovered that each flower represented a different creature. The Friendship Garden, as it was called, was a symbol of the bonds formed between the meadow's inhabitants. Buzzy realized that to create strong and lasting friendships; he would need to plant seeds of kindness, understanding, and compassion.

His first challenge was figuring out how to approach the garden's flowers without harming them. Buzzy had to learn to approach each flower gently, taking care not to damage the delicate petals, just as he would need to treat potential friends with care and respect.

Buzzy soon met a charming butterfly named Bloom, who fluttered among the Friendship Garden's blossoms. Bloom showed Buzzy how to nurture each friendship flower by giving it sunlight, water, and nutrients. These acts of care and attention represented the time and effort it took to maintain a strong bond between friends.

As Buzzy continued to explore the Friendship Garden, he encountered a young turtle named Sheldon. Sheldon taught Buzzy the importance of patience and resilience in cultivating friendships. Like the flowers in the garden, friendships require time to grow and could face challenges, such as droughts or storms. By standing together through difficult times, friends could grow even stronger.

Buzzy spent the day tending to the Friendship Garden, learning valuable lessons from each new friend he made. As the sun began to set, he noticed that the garden had grown even more beautiful and diverse, thanks to the care he and his new friends had given it.

Buzzy flew back to his colony with a heart of gratitude, eager to share his lessons. He understood that friendships, like flowers, needed nurturing, patience, and resilience to thrive. And just as the garden bloomed with various flowers, Buzzy's life was now enriched by the unique and diverse friendships he had formed.

From that day forward, Buzzy dedicated himself to his work in the meadow and nurturing the friendships he had made. The garden continued to grow and flourish, a symbol of everlasting friendship.

Lessons Revealed

Healing metaphor: The metaphor in this story lies in the Friendship Garden and the process of nurturing the flowers, which represents building and maintaining friendships through acts of kindness, understanding, and compassion, as well as the importance of patience and resilience in overcoming challenges and fostering strong and diverse connections with others.

Importance of friendships: The story demonstrates the value of forming and nurturing diverse friendships. Children can learn that building connections with others enriches their lives and contributes to a supportive community.

Patience and resilience: Buzzy learns from Sheldon that friendships require time, patience, and resilience. Children can apply this lesson to their relationships, understanding that friendships can face challenges and require effort to grow stronger.

Care and respect: Buzzy learns to approach the flowers gently, symbolizing the care and respect needed when interacting with friends. This teaches children the importance of treating others with kindness and consideration.

Nurturing relationships: Bloom shows Buzzy how to care for the Friendship Garden, representing the time and effort needed to maintain healthy friendships. Children can learn that investing time and attention in their relationships can lead to strong, lasting bonds.

Appreciating diversity: The Friendship Garden is home to a variety of flowers, symbolizing the diverse friendships Buzzy forms. This can help children understand and appreciate the beauty of diversity in their friendships and broader communities.

Suggested Activities

Friendship garden art: Have children create their own Friendship Garden using art materials like paint, crayons, or collage materials. Encourage them to include representations of their friends, emphasizing the unique qualities each friend brings to their life.

Caring for friendship: Discuss the importance of nurturing friendships by showing kindness, understanding, and compassion. Have them brainstorm ways to care for their friendships, such as spending time together, listening, and offering help when needed.

Role-playing: Organize role-playing activities that demonstrate positive friendship behaviors, such as empathy, sharing, and conflict resolution. This activity can help children develop essential social skills and practice maintaining healthy relationships.

Friendship flower pot: Provide children with small flower pots and let them decorate them with symbols of friendship. They can plant seeds in the pots and care for the plants as a metaphor for caring for their friendships.

Storytelling: Encourage children to share stories of their own friendships, focusing on the qualities they appreciate in their friends and the memorable experiences they have shared.

Building resilience: Discuss with children the importance of patience and friendship resilience. Help them think of times they have faced challenges with friends and how they overcame those obstacles together.

Friendship chain: Create a paper chain with each link representing a friend or a positive quality of a good friend. Display the chain in the classroom or at home as a visual reminder of the importance of friendships.

Acts of kindness: Have children brainstorm acts of kindness they can do for their friends or classmates. Encourage them to perform these acts and discuss the impact it has on their friendships.

Friendship journal: Provide children with journals to write about their friendships, including the qualities they admire in their friends and the activities they enjoy doing together.

Story extension: Invite children to write or draw their own continuation of Buzzy's story, highlighting how he continues to develop and maintain friendships in the meadow.

"Friendship Flower Pot" Activity

The Friendship Flower Pot activity is a creative and fun way to help children think about the qualities of a good friend and express their appreciation for their friends. In this activity, children will decorate a flower pot and create flowers representing the qualities they appreciate in their friends.

Materials:

- Small terra cotta flower pots (one for each child)
- Acrylic paint, markers, or colored pencils
- Paintbrushes (if using paint)
- Construction paper or card stock in various colors
- Scissors
- Glue or tape
- Green pipe cleaners or straws
- Optional: soil and flower seeds

Instructions:

1. Provide each child with a small terra cotta flower pot. Explain that they will be decorating the pot to represent their friendship and the qualities they appreciate in their friends.

2. Allow children to decorate their flower pots using acrylic paint, markers, or colored pencils. Encourage them to be creative and use colors, patterns, and designs that represent their friendships or the qualities they appreciate in their friends.

3. While the flower pots dry, provide children with construction paper or card stock in various colors. Instruct them to draw and cut out flower shapes, with each flower representing a quality they appreciate in a friend (e.g., kindness, loyalty, humor).

4. Have the children write or draw the quality they appreciate in their friends on each flower.

5. Attach a green pipe cleaner or straw to the back of each flower using glue or tape. These will act as the stems for the flowers.

6. Once the flower pots are dry and the flowers are complete, have the children place the flower stems into their pots, creating a bouquet of friendship qualities.

7. Optional: Provide soil and flower seeds for the children to plant in their decorated flower pots. This can symbolize the growth and nurturing of friendships.

Encourage children to share their friendship flower pots with their peers or family members, discussing the qualities they appreciate in their friends and the importance of nurturing and supporting friendships. This activity promotes self-expression, creativity, and a deeper understanding of being a good friend.

6

Cammie's True Colors

Peer pressure, embracing individuality, importance of true friendships,
self-confidence, self-acceptance, seeking wise counsel

Once upon a time, a young chameleon named Cammie lived in a vibrant forest filled with colorful creatures. Cammie was known for changing colors and blending in with her surroundings. She was a cheerful and friendly chameleon who enjoyed exploring the forest and meeting new friends.

One day, Cammie came across a group of animals called the "Cool Crew," known for being the most popular animals in the forest. They were Lenny the Lion, Zane the Zebra, and Freddy the Flamingo. Cammie was in awe of the Cool Crew and longed to be friends with them.

When she approached them, Lenny the Lion said, "If you want to be friends with us, Cammie, you need to prove that you're as cool as we are."

Eager to fit in, Cammie asked, "What do I need to do?" Zane the Zebra said, "First, you must change your colors to match ours. Lions are golden, zebras have black and white stripes, and flamingos are pink. Pick one and change into that color."

Cammie hesitated but eventually changed her colors to match Freddy the Flamingo's vibrant pink. The Cool Crew seemed impressed, but they had more challenges for her. They asked Cammie to mimic their voices, change her way of walking, and even play pranks on other animals in the forest.

Cammie did everything they asked, but deep down, she felt unhappy. She missed her own colors, her own voice, and her old friends who genuinely cared about her.

One day, as Cammie was sitting by a pond, she met a frog named Oliver. Oliver was gentle and kind-hearted. He noticed Cammie's sadness and asked her what was wrong.

Cammie told Oliver about the Cool Crew and how she had changed herself to fit in. Oliver listened carefully and said, "Cammie, true friends will accept you for who you are. You don't need to change to please others. Be true to yourself, and you'll find the friends that truly matter."

Cammie realized that Oliver was right. She embraced her unique colors and voice once again and promised to stop playing pranks on others. When she returned to the Cool Crew, they were surprised by her transformation.

Lenny the Lion asked, "Why did you change back, Cammie? Don't you want to be part of our group?"

Cammie replied, "I realized I do not need to change who I am to fit in. I want to be friends with those who accept me for who I am."

Over time, Cammie reconnected with her old friends and even made new ones who loved her for her unique qualities. She learned that being true to herself was far more important than trying to fit in with others. And in the end, by embracing her authentic self, Cammie the Chameleon became one of the happiest and most confident creatures in the forest.

Lessons Revealed

Healing metaphor: The metaphor in this story lies in Cammie's color-changing ability, which represents her efforts to change her personality, appearance, and behavior to fit in with the Cool Crew. This symbolizes the pressure people may feel to conform to social norms or expectations to be accepted, ultimately discovering that true friendships and happiness come from being authentic to oneself.

Embracing individuality: The story shows how Cammie learns the importance of being true to herself and embracing her unique qualities. This can help children understand that they do not need to change to fit in or please others.

Importance of true friendships: Cammie discovers that true friends will accept her for who she is rather than expecting her to change. This can help children recognize the value of having friends who support and appreciate their individuality.

Self-confidence and self-acceptance: Through her journey, Cammie gains confidence in her own identity and learns to accept herself as she is. This can encourage children to develop self-confidence and self-acceptance, fostering a positive self-image.

Peer pressure and resilience: Cammie faces peer pressure from the Cool Crew to change herself to be accepted. The story can help children understand the potential consequences of giving in to peer pressure and teach them resilience in the face of such challenges.

Seeking wise counsel: Cammie's encounter with Oliver helps her realize the importance of staying true to herself. This can teach children the value of seeking advice from wise and trusted individuals when facing difficult situations.

Suggested Activities

Colorful self-portrait: Have children create self-portraits using their favorite colors and materials. Encourage them to include elements that represent their unique qualities, interests, and personality.

True friends discussion: Discuss the qualities of true friends, such as acceptance, support, and kindness. Ask them to think about their own friends and how they demonstrate these qualities.

Role-playing: Organize role-playing activities that teach children about peer pressure and the importance of staying true to themselves. This activity can help children practice standing up for themselves and recognizing the value of their unique qualities.

Storytelling: Encourage children to share stories about times when they stayed true to themselves, even in challenging situations. Discuss the importance of self-confidence and self-acceptance.

Positive affirmations: Help children create a list of positive affirmations about themselves, focusing on their unique qualities and strengths. Encourage them to repeat these affirmations regularly to build self-confidence.

Building a supportive community: Collaborate with children to create a classroom or home environment where everyone feels accepted and valued. Encourage children to celebrate each other's unique qualities and support one another.

Peer pressure scenarios: Present children with scenarios involving peer pressure and discuss how they can handle these situations while staying true to themselves. This activity can help children develop decision-making skills and confidence in handling challenging social situations.

Circle of support: Encourage children to identify their support network, including friends, family members, and other trusted individuals who accept and care for them. Discuss the importance of maintaining these supportive relationships.

Gratitude journal: Provide children with journals to write about their friendships, focusing on the qualities they appreciate in their friends and moments of support and acceptance.

"Peer Pressure" Activity

The Peer Pressure Scenarios activity is designed to help children understand the concept of peer pressure and practice making positive choices in various situations. By discussing and role-playing scenarios, children can develop strategies for handling peer pressure and staying true to their values.

Materials:

- Index cards or small pieces of paper
- Pens or pencils
- Optional: a small box or container to hold the scenario cards

Instructions:

1. Prepare several index cards or small pieces of paper with different peer pressure scenarios written on them. These scenarios should involve situations where children might feel pressured to conform or make choices that go against their values. Some examples include: (a) a friend wants you to cheat on a test, (b) a group of kids is making fun of someone, and they want you to join in.

2. Gather the children in a circle or a comfortable seating arrangement. Explain the concept of peer pressure and discuss how it can sometimes lead to making choices that go against their values or what they know is right.

3. Introduce the Peer Pressure Scenarios activity. Explain that you will be presenting scenarios, and the children will take turns discussing or acting out how they would handle the situation.

4. Place the prepared cards in a small box or container. Have one child pick a card and read the scenario aloud. Encourage the child to share their thoughts on how they would handle the situation.

5. Invite other children to offer their ideas and suggestions as well. This will create an open discussion and allow the children to learn from one another.

6. Once everyone has had a chance to contribute, move on to the next scenario. Repeat until all scenarios have been discussed.

7. To conclude the activity, discuss the importance of staying true to their values and making positive choices, even when faced with peer pressure.

This activity promotes critical thinking, problem-solving, and empathy as children learn to navigate challenging social situations and stay true to their values. By practicing these skills in a supportive environment, children can build the confidence and resilience needed to face peer pressure in their everyday lives.

7

Rosie's Garden of Growth

Overcoming shyness, importance of taking small steps, encouragement from supportive friends, inner strength, embracing new experiences

In a small, peaceful garden, a tiny roly-poly named Rosie called this cozy patch of soil home. Rosie was a shy and gentle creature who loved to explore the wonders of her garden home. However, whenever she encountered something new, Rosie would curl up into a tight ball, just like a tiny pebble, to protect herself.

Rosie had many friends in the garden, including an old snail called Shimmer, who had noticed her shyness. Shimmer had seen many creatures come and go in his long life and learned that facing fears was necessary for personal growth.

One sunny day, Shimmer gathered the courage to share his wisdom with Rosie. "Rosie," he began, "you are a lovely roly-poly, but

I've noticed that you often hide when you're afraid. You know, it's okay to be cautious, but you'll miss out on life's beautiful experiences if you always curl up into a ball."

Rosie listened intently, and Shimmer's words resonated with her. She would face her fears and overcome her shyness with Shimmer's guidance. He suggested she start small by approaching a gentle earthworm named Wiggles, who lived nearby.

Rosie hesitated, but remembering Shimmer's advice, she bravely approached Wiggles. To her delight, Wiggles was kind and friendly, and they quickly became friends. This small act of courage made Rosie feel more confident, and she decided to continue her journey of self-discovery.

Rosie's next challenge was to cross a small, babbling brook that ran through the garden. Though the water was shallow, the sound of the flowing water and the sight of the unfamiliar terrain frightened her. Rosie remembered how she had faced her fear with Wiggles, and, taking a deep breath; she slowly made her way across the pebbles that lined the brook's edge.

With each successful step, Rosie felt her shyness receding like a wave, replaced by newfound confidence and strength. She realized that her shell was not only for protection but also a symbol of her resilience and inner strength.

As the days passed, Rosie continued to face her fears and embrace new experiences. She explored the highest branches of the trees, danced with the butterflies, and even met a friendly beetle. She found that the more she embraced the unknown, the more her world expanded, and the less she felt the need to curl up into a ball.

Rosie's journey taught her that shyness could be overcome by facing her fears, one small step at a time. Her once-limiting shell now symbolized her strength and resilience, and she became an inspiration to all the creatures in the garden.

And so, Rosie the roly-poly transformed from a timid creature into a brave and adventurous soul because she dared to step out of her shell and embrace the world around her.

Lessons Revealed

Healing metaphor: The metaphor in this story is Rosie's habit of curling up into a ball when she is frightened, representing how people may withdraw or isolate themselves when facing fears or difficult situations. As Rosie faces her fears and gains confidence, her shell becomes a symbol of her strength and resilience, illustrating the personal growth that can come from confronting one's fears and embracing new experiences.

Overcoming shyness: The story follows Rosie's journey as she learns to face her fears and overcome her shyness. This can help children understand that working through their fears and becoming more confident in unfamiliar situations is possible.

Importance of taking small steps: Rosie learns that taking small steps and facing her fears gradually can lead to personal growth. This can teach children that they don't need to tackle their fears all at once; instead, they can approach them step by step.

Encouragement from supportive friends: Shimmer's guidance and encouragement play a significant role in helping Rosie overcome her shyness. This can teach children the importance of having supportive friends who can help them grow and face their fears.

Resilience and inner strength: As Rosie faces her fears, she realizes that her shell is not just for protection but also represents her resilience and inner strength. This can inspire children to recognize their own inner strength and resilience when facing challenges.

Exploration and embracing new experiences: Rosie's journey encourages her to explore new areas and embrace new experiences. This can help children understand the value of stepping out of their comfort zones and embracing the world around them.

Suggested Activities

Fear ladder: Help children create a fear ladder by listing their fears from least to most frightening. Encourage them to face each fear gradually, just like Rosie, to build confidence and resilience.

Role-playing: Organize role-playing activities that teach children how to handle various situations that may cause anxiety or fear. This activity can help them develop coping skills and build confidence.

Story extension: Invite children to write or draw their own continuation of Rosie's story, exploring how she continues to face her fears and grow in confidence.

Support system: Encourage children to identify their support network, including friends, family members, and other trusted individuals who can help them face their fears, just like Shimmer helped Rosie.

Courage collage: Create a collage using images, words, and phrases representing courage, resilience, and personal growth.

Discussion: Talk with children about the importance of facing their fears and stepping out of their comfort zones. Share stories of when you or others overcame fears and experienced personal growth.

Affirmations: Help children create a list of positive affirmations related to courage, strength, and resilience. Encourage them to repeat these affirmations regularly to build self-confidence.

Mindfulness and relaxation techniques: Teach children mindfulness and relaxation techniques, such as deep breathing or visualization, to help them manage their fears and anxiety.

Group activities: Organize group activities where children can practice facing their fears in a supportive environment. This can help them build confidence and develop social skills.

"Fear Ladder" Activity

The Fear Ladder activity is designed to help children understand their fears and anxieties and develop strategies to face and overcome them. By breaking down fears into smaller steps and practicing gradual exposure, children can build confidence and resilience in overcoming challenges.

Materials:

- Large sheet of paper or poster board
- Markers or colored pencils
- Ruler or straight edge (optional)

Instructions:

1. Begin by discussing the concept of fears and anxieties with the children. Explain that everyone experiences fear and that feeling scared or nervous about certain things is normal. Discuss how facing fears can help us grow and become more confident.

2. Introduce the Fear Ladder activity. Explain that the purpose of this activity is to create a visual representation of their fears, broken down into smaller steps that they can work through to overcome their fear eventually.

3. Provide each child with a large sheet of paper, poster board, markers, or colored pencils. If desired, help them draw a ladder on the paper using a ruler or straight edge. The ladder should have several rungs, with enough space to write on each one.

4. Instruct the children to think of a specific fear they would like to overcome. This could be anything from speaking to the class to trying a new activity or making new friends. Have them write their fear at the top of the ladder.

5. Next, guide the children in breaking down their fear into smaller, more manageable steps. Each step should represent a slightly less challenging or anxiety-provoking situation related to their fear. Have them write each step on a separate rung of the ladder, starting from the bottom with the least anxiety-provoking step and working their way up.

6. Once the Fear Ladder is complete, discuss how they can use this tool to practice facing their fears. Encourage the children to start with the lowest rung and gradually move up the ladder as they become more comfortable and confident.

7. Provide support and encouragement as the children work through their Fear Ladders. Check-in with them periodically to discuss their progress and celebrate their accomplishments.

The Fear Ladder activity encourages children to confront and overcome their fears gradually and systematically. By breaking down fears into smaller steps and practicing gradual exposure, children can build confidence and resilience in facing and overcoming challenges.

8

Hope's Healing Heart

Importance of kindness and compassion, the power of hope and healing, the impact of one's actions on others, overcoming challenges, beauty in diversity

High above the rolling hills, a rainbow of colors could be seen as Hope, a striking butterfly, soared through the sky. She was no ordinary butterfly; her mesmerizing and colorful wings shimmered in the sunlight and could brighten the darkest of days.

In the heart of the countryside, a lush garden bloomed with brilliant flowers. These flowers came in all shapes, sizes, and colors, and their distinct scents mingled together to create a symphony of fragrances. The garden was always alive with the buzzing of bees, the fluttering of butterflies, and the melodic songs of birds.

Hope the butterfly knew she had a unique gift. Whenever she spread her wings and soared above the garden, a sparkling, golden dust trail would follow, gently falling onto the flowers below. This magical dust had the power to heal and rejuvenate the most wilted and withered flowers, restoring their natural radiance and vitality.

One sunny day, Hope discovered a small, secluded corner of the garden where the flowers appeared drooping, their once-vibrant colors faded and dull.

Among these flowers was a bluebell named Melancholy, who struggled the most. Melancholy had lost its luster and stood with its head bowed low, shrouded in shadows.

Moved by compassion, Hope fluttered gracefully towards Melancholy, guided by the desire to alleviate its suffering. As the gentle breeze carried the golden dust toward the bluebell, it began to sway ever so slightly. The healing dust enveloped Melancholy, and almost instantly, the flower's true essence started to reemerge.

With every brush of Hope's wings, Melancholy's petals became more vibrant, and its head began to lift higher and higher. The shadows that once consumed the flower receded, replaced by the sunlight's warm, comforting embrace. Melancholy felt a renewed sense of strength and vitality, and the world around it transformed into a more inviting and nurturing place.

The other flowers in the garden witnessed this beautiful transition, and they, too, felt a renewed sense of purpose. As Hope continued to spread her wings and shower the garden with her magical dust, the once-drooping flowers began to flourish and reach for the sky, creating a breathtaking canvas of color and life.

And so, the garden continued to thrive, becoming a sanctuary for all who sought comfort and healing. Hope the butterfly, with her miraculous touch, taught the flowers that even in the darkest corners, there is always light and the promise of a brighter tomorrow.

Lessons Revealed

Healing metaphor: The metaphor revolves around Hope, the butterfly with magical healing dust, and Melancholy, the wilted bluebell. The healing dust symbolizes the transformative influence of hope and kindness, while Melancholy represents those struggling emotionally. The story represents the power of hope and positive energy in helping others with their struggles and emotional pain.

Importance of kindness and compassion: Hope's willingness to help Melancholy demonstrates the significance of empathy and compassion. This story can teach children the value of being kind and considerate toward others struggling or needing support.

The power of hope and healing: Hope's magical dust represents the healing power of hope and positivity. The story can help children understand that even in difficult situations, having hope and a positive attitude can make a significant difference in their lives and the lives of others.

The impact of one's actions on others: As Hope helps Melancholy, the other flowers in the garden also benefit from her actions. This can teach children that their actions can have a ripple effect, influencing the well-being of those around them.

Overcoming challenges: Melancholy's transformation shows that even when facing challenges, it is possible to overcome them with the right support and encouragement. This can help children learn to persevere and thrive despite life's obstacles.

Beauty in diversity: The story highlights the diversity of the garden, with flowers of various shapes, sizes, and colors. This can teach children to appreciate and celebrate the beauty in diversity, both in nature and among people.

Suggested Activities

Emotional expression: Encourage children to discuss or draw pictures of their feelings, both positive and negative, and to share how these emotions affect their daily lives. This helps children identify and express their feelings effectively.

Plant a seed of hope: Have children plant a seed and take care of it, using this activity as a metaphor for nurturing hope and healing in their own lives. Discuss how their care helps the plant grow and how self-care can help them grow emotionally.

Healing artwork: Invite children to create artwork representing healing, hope, and positive change. This activity encourages self-expression and helps children visualize their journey toward emotional well-being.

Story extension: Ask children to write or draw their own continuation of the story, exploring how Hope's healing touch affects the other flowers and creatures in the garden. This activity helps children imagine positive outcomes for their own emotional healing.

Role-playing: Organize role-playing activities that teach children how to support others struggling emotionally. This helps children develop empathy and learn how to be a source of comfort for their friends and loved ones.

Acts of kindness: Encourage children to perform acts of kindness for others, both within and outside their families, to create a positive impact and spread hope and healing in their community.

Gratitude journal: Provide children with a journal to record things they are grateful for each day. Practicing gratitude helps children focus on the positives in their lives and fosters a sense of happiness and well-being.

Group discussions: Organize group discussions where children can share their experiences, emotions, and ideas related to hope, healing, and personal growth. This provides a supportive environment for children to express themselves and learn from others' experiences.

Mindfulness and relaxation techniques: Teach children mindfulness and relaxation techniques, such as deep breathing or guided imagery, to help them cope with negative emotions and promote emotional healing.

"Gratitude Journal" Activity

The Gratitude Journal activity is designed to help children develop a habit of focusing on the positive aspects of their lives, fostering a greater sense of appreciation and happiness. By regularly writing down things they are grateful for, children can cultivate a more positive mindset and build resilience during challenging times.

Materials:

- Notebook or journal (one for each child)
- Pens or pencils
- Optional: stickers, colored pencils, or markers for decoration

Instructions:

1. Begin by discussing the concept of gratitude with the children. Explain that gratitude means being thankful and appreciative of the good things in our lives, whether big or small. Talk about the benefits of practicing gratitude, such as increased happiness, improved well-being, and a greater ability to cope with stress.
2. Introduce the Gratitude Journal activity. Explain that the purpose of this activity is to create a daily habit of reflecting on and writing down things they are grateful for. This will help them focus on the positive aspects of their lives and cultivate a greater sense of appreciation and happiness.
3. Provide each child with a notebook or journal and a pen or pencil. If desired, allow them to decorate their journal with stickers, colored pencils, or markers to make it personal and inviting.
4. Guide the children through the process of creating their first gratitude journal entry. Encourage them to think of three things they are grateful for that day. It could be something as simple as a sunny day or a kind word from a friend, or something more significant like a supportive family or achieving a personal goal.
5. Instruct the children to write down their three things in their journal and explain why they are grateful for each one. Encourage them to be specific and thoughtful in their explanations.

6. As the children become more comfortable with the activity, encourage them to expand their gratitude practice by writing down more items, exploring different areas of their lives, or reflecting on their gratitude in greater depth.

7. Set aside time each day or week for the children to update their Gratitude Journals. Establishing a routine will help them develop the habit of practicing gratitude consistently.

8. Periodically, discuss the children's progress with their Gratitude Journals. Encourage them to share their experiences, discuss challenges they may have faced, and celebrate their accomplishments.

The Gratitude Journal activity helps children focus on the positive aspects of their lives, fostering a greater sense of appreciation and happiness. Children can cultivate a more positive mindset and build resilience during challenging times by regularly writing down things they are grateful for.

9

Holly's New Home

Embracing change, overcoming fears and challenges, the value of perseverance, seeking help and wisdom from others, supporting others

Holly the Hermit Crab scurried across the sandy floor of her tide pool home, her shell clanging against the rocks as she searched for food. The ocean was Holly's playground, and she spent her days investigating the nooks and crannies of the rocky landscape, always eager to discover something new.

One sunny day, Holly noticed that her shell was beginning to feel tight and uncomfortable. She realized she had been growing and needed a larger shell to accommodate her changing body. This realization brought about a mix of emotions in Holly, as she felt excited about her growth and apprehensive about leaving her familiar home behind.

Holly encountered a starfish named Sandy as she embarked on her quest for a new shell. Sensing Holly's uncertainty, Sandy shared a wise lesson with her: "Holly, my dear, growth and change are much like the ever-shifting tides. Just as the tides rise and fall, change is a natural part of life. Embrace it, and you'll find that each wave brings a new opportunity for growth and happiness."

Inspired by Sandy's wisdom, Holly bravely searched for a new shell. Along the way, she encountered many challenges, such as strong currents and predators. Each time she faced an obstacle, she remembered Sandy's words and found the strength to continue.

As Holly continued her search, she came across a narrow passage between two large rocks. From the other side, she could see the

reflection of a beautiful shell that seemed perfect for her. However, the path was lined with sharp, jagged edges that threatened to damage her fragile body if she attempted to squeeze through.

Holly hesitated, considering the risk. She knew that finding the right shell was important, but she also feared the potential harm she might face. Holly remembered Sandy's wise words about embracing change and finding strength in adversity. With a deep breath, she mustered the courage to tackle the challenge ahead.

Carefully, Holly began her delicate journey through the dangerous passage. She moved slowly, using her legs to carefully navigate the sharp rocks, while her antennae helped her sense the safest path forward. With determination and perseverance, Holly managed to avoid harm and finally emerged on the other side, triumphant.

The beautiful shell was even more stunning up close. Although the journey had been difficult and fraught with challenges, Holly knew overcoming her fears and pushing through the obstacle was worth it. She was one step closer to finding her perfect new home, and she felt a sense of pride in her ability to face adversity head-on.

As the tides continued to ebb and flow, Holly the Hermit Crab lived a happy and fulfilling life, always ready to adapt and thrive in the face of change. With her newfound wisdom, Holly became a source of inspiration for the other creatures in the tide pool. She shared her story and the lessons she had learned, helping her friends embrace the changes in their own lives.

Lessons Revealed

Healing metaphor: The metaphor in this story revolves around Holly, the Hermit Crab who needs a new shell, and her journey to find one. Holly's old shell symbolizes the familiar and comfortable aspects of life that people might be hesitant to leave behind, while the new shell represents the opportunities and possibilities that come with embracing change. The story represents the challenges and fears individuals face when they need to adapt to change, grow, and move forward in life.

Embracing change: Holly's search for a new shell teaches children that change is a natural part of life. This story can help them understand that they may experience growth and changes, leading to new opportunities and experiences.

Overcoming fears and challenges: Holly's journey through the narrow passage demonstrates that facing fears and challenges can lead to personal growth. This can inspire children to confront their own fears and difficulties with courage and determination.

The value of perseverance: Holly's determination to find a new shell, despite the challenges she encounters, highlights the importance of perseverance. This story can encourage children to keep trying, even when facing obstacles or setbacks.

Seeking help and wisdom from others: Holly listens to Sandy's advice and finds strength in his wisdom. This can teach children the value of seeking guidance from others, such as parents, teachers, or friends when facing challenges or making important decisions.

Supporting others: As Holly shares her story and lessons with her friends, she helps them embrace changes in their lives. This can teach children the importance of offering support and encouragement to others facing challenges or uncertainties.

Suggested Activities

Share your own story: Encourage children to discuss their experiences with change and growth. This activity helps children relate to Holly's story and explore their feelings about change.

Create a change collage: Ask children to make a collage using pictures, drawings, or words that represent changes they have experienced or would like to experience. This activity helps children visualize and understand the concept of change.

Role-playing: Organize role-playing activities where children can practice coping with change and overcoming challenges. This helps children develop problem-solving skills and build resilience.

Facing fears: Encourage children to identify their fears related to change and discuss ways to overcome them. This activity helps children develop strategies for managing their fears and anxieties.

Story extension: Invite children to write or draw a continuation of Holly's story, exploring how she adapts to her new shell and how her growth impacts her life. This activity helps children imagine positive outcomes for their own experiences of change.

Growth mindset: Discuss the concept of a growth mindset with children, emphasizing the importance of embracing change and learning from challenges.

Embracing change journal: Provide children with a journal to record their experiences with change, including challenges they have faced and how they have grown from these experiences. This activity helps children reflect on their own personal growth and can help build self-awareness.

Group discussions: Organize group discussions where children can share their thoughts and feelings about change, growth, and facing challenges. This provides a supportive environment for children to express themselves and learn from others' experiences.

Lessons from nature: Discuss how animals and plants adapt to change and explore the lessons we can learn from nature. This activity helps children understand that change is a natural part of life.

Create a change poem: Invite children to write a poem about change, growth, and overcoming challenges. This activity encourages self-expression and helps children process their feelings about change in a creative way.

"Create a Change Poem" Activity

The Create a Change Poem activity is designed to help children explore and express their feelings about change and transition. By creating their poems, children can develop a deeper understanding of their emotions, learn to cope with change healthily and build empathy for others experiencing similar situations.

Materials:

- Paper
- Pens or pencils
- Optional: colored pencils or markers for decoration

Instructions:

1. Begin by discussing the concept of change with the children. Share examples of changes they might experience, such as moving to a new home, starting a new school, or making new friends. Talk about how change is a natural part of life, and it can be both exciting and challenging.

2. Introduce the Create a Change Poem activity. Explain that the purpose of this activity is to help them explore their feelings about change through poetry. Encourage them to think about a change they have experienced or one they might face in the future.

3. Provide each child with paper and a pen or pencil. If desired, allow them to use colored pencils or markers to decorate their paper and make their poem visually appealing.

4. Guide the children through the process of brainstorming ideas for their poems. Encourage them to think about the emotions they experienced or might experience during a change, the challenges they faced, and the positive aspects of the change.

5. Help the children structure their poems using a simple format, such as an acrostic poem, a rhyming poem, or a free-verse poem:

• Acrostic Poem: Write the word "CHANGE" vertically down the left side of the paper. For each letter, write a word or phrase that relates to change, starting with that letter.

• Rhyming Poem: Write a poem with a simple rhyme scheme to describe their feelings about change.

• Free-Verse Poem: Write a poem without a specific structure or rhyme scheme, focusing on the emotions and experiences associated with change.

6. Give the children time to write their poems, offering assistance and encouragement as needed. Encourage them to be creative and express their feelings honestly.

7. Once the children have completed their poems, provide an opportunity for them to share their work with the group. Encourage them to discuss their poems, explaining the emotions and experiences they described in their writing.

8. Reflect on the activity, discussing the different emotions and experiences the children shared in their poems. Emphasize the importance of understanding and managing feelings during times of change and the value of empathy for others experiencing similar situations.

The Create a Change Poem activity helps children explore and express their feelings about change and transition, develop a deeper understanding of their emotions, and build empathy for others experiencing similar situations.

10

Embracing Our Unique Feathers

Self-esteem, building self-confidence, embracing individuality, empathy and understanding, overcoming insecurities

Apeacock named Pluma, known for her wisdom and beauty, lived in the heart of a lush and enchanting forest. Pluma's mesmerizing feathers shimmered with a thousand hues as the sunlight glistened against them.

In this same forest, a young bird named Flutter struggled to accept her appearance. Flutter's small and ordinary feathers paled compared to the other birds' bright colors. Feeling inadequate, she spent her days hidden away, afraid to reveal her true self to the world.

One summer day, as Flutter watched from behind a bush, Pluma elegantly strolled through the forest, her bright feathers captivating everyone's attention.

Flutter couldn't help but marvel at Pluma's confidence, yearning to possess such radiance and self-assurance.

Sensing Flutter's presence, Pluma approached the bush and gently asked, "Why are you hiding, little bird?" Flutter hesitated before emerging from her hiding spot; her head hung low.

"I'm ashamed of my plain feathers," Flutter confessed. "I wish I were as beautiful and confident as you, Pluma."

Pluma smiled warmly at Flutter. "My dear, beauty comes in many forms, and each of us possesses unique qualities to celebrate. Let me show you something."

Pluma guided Flutter to a nearby clearing, where they discovered a crystal-clear pond. As they gazed at their reflections, Pluma unfurled Flutter's wings, unveiling an array of hidden colors within her feathers.

"Look closely, Flutter. Can you see the delicate beauty in your feathers? The gentle gradients of color, the intricate patterns? You are just as beautiful as any other bird in this forest."

Flutter's eyes widened in wonder as she realized that Pluma was right. Though not as bright and flashy as Pluma's, her feathers held their own unique allure.

"Pluma," Flutter asked hesitantly, "have you always been so confident?"

Pluma looked at her thoughtfully before responding. "You know, Flutter, there was a time when I, too, struggled to accept my own unique appearance."

Flutter's eyes widened with surprise as she listened intently.

"When I was young," Pluma continued, "my colorful feathers made me stand out among my peers, and I often felt like an outsider. I was teased for being different, leading to doubts and insecurities."

As Pluma shared her story, the fireflies gathered around, casting a soft glow on the two friends.

"I started to hide my true self, tucking my vibrant feathers beneath dull, ordinary ones, just to blend in," Pluma confessed. "But one day, my mother took notice and offered some life-changing advice. She told me that my feathers were a gift, that their vibrancy reflected the beauty within me."

Flutter listened, her heart swelling with admiration for her friend's courage and resilience.

"Remember, dear Flutter, every creature has its own journey and struggles with self-acceptance. But when we learn to love and embrace our unique qualities, we can truly shine and inspire others to do the same."

Flutter felt an even deeper connection to her new friend as they sat beneath the stars. She was grateful for their bond and the lessons of self-acceptance they had learned, knowing they would carry this wisdom with them for the rest of their lives.

Lessons Revealed

Healing metaphor: The metaphor in this story revolves around the self-acceptance journey of two birds, Pluma and Flutter, who both struggled with their appearance. Pluma's vibrant and radiant feathers represent the external beauty many admire and desire. On the other hand, Flutter's small and ordinary feathers symbolize the perceived inadequacies that individuals might feel about their own appearance or abilities.

Embracing individuality: The story of Pluma and Flutter highlights the importance of embracing one's unique qualities and celebrating individuality. Children can learn that everyone has their own special characteristics and there is beauty in diversity.

Building self-confidence: Flutter's journey to self-acceptance shows children that self-confidence can grow by acknowledging and valuing one's unique attributes. This can encourage them to develop healthy self-esteem and be proud of themselves.

Empathy and understanding: Pluma's willingness to share her own experiences with self-doubt and insecurity can teach children the value of empathy and understanding. By recognizing that everyone faces challenges and self-doubt, children can learn to be more compassionate and supportive of others.

The power of friendship: Pluma's friendship and guidance help Flutter see the beauty within herself. This story can demonstrate the positive impact that friendships can have on personal growth and emotional well-being.

Overcoming insecurities: The story illustrates that it is possible to overcome insecurities and self-doubt by focusing on one's inner strengths and unique qualities. This can encourage children to face their insecurities and work towards self-acceptance.

Suggested Activities

Self-reflection: Encourage children to discuss and share their unique qualities and how these make them special. This activity promotes self-awareness and self-acceptance.

Create a "Unique Me" collage: Invite children to create a collage representing their individuality and uniqueness using pictures, drawings, or words.

Compliment circle: Create a compliment circle where children take turns sharing positive qualities they appreciate about their peers. This activity fosters a supportive and encouraging environment.

Role-playing: Set up role-playing scenarios where children can practice building self-esteem and confidence by embracing their unique qualities. This helps develop social skills and self-assurance.

Story extension: Encourage children to write or draw a continuation of Pluma and Flutter's story, exploring how they spread their message of self-acceptance to other animals in the forest. This activity inspires creative thinking and empathy.

Group discussions: Facilitate group discussions where children can share their thoughts and feelings about self-acceptance, individuality, and celebrating differences. This provides a supportive environment for children to express themselves and learn from others' experiences.

Embracing diversity: Discuss with children the importance of embracing and celebrating diversity in all its forms, using examples from the natural world and human societies. This activity helps children understand the value of diversity and promotes tolerance.

Create a "Self-Love" poem: Ask children to write a poem about self-acceptance, self-love, and embracing their unique qualities. This encourages self-expression and fosters a positive self-image.

Acts of kindness: Encourage children to perform acts of kindness for others, particularly those who may be struggling with self-acceptance or feeling different. This activity promotes empathy and compassion.

"Unique Me Collage" Activity

The Create a "Unique Me" Collage activity allows children to explore and celebrate their uniqueness and individuality. By creating a collage filled with images, words, and symbols representing their interests, talents, and qualities, children can develop a greater appreciation for their individuality and the diversity of their peers.

Materials:

- Construction paper or poster board (for the collage background)
- Magazines, newspapers, or printed images
- Scissors
- Glue or glue sticks
- Markers or colored pencils
- Optional: stickers, masking tape, or other decorative items

Instructions:

1. Begin by discussing the concept of uniqueness and individuality with the children. Talk about how each person is special in their own way and that embracing and celebrating our differences is important.

2. Introduce the Create a Unique Me Collage activity. Explain that this activity aims to help them explore and express their individuality through a visual representation of their interests, talents, and qualities.

3. Provide each child with a piece of construction paper or poster board as the background for their collage. Encourage them to choose a color that they feel represents their personality or that they like.

4. Have the children look through magazines, newspapers, or printed images to find pictures and words that represent their interests, talents, and qualities. They can also draw or write their own images and words using markers or colored pencils.

5. Encourage the children to consider what makes them unique and special, such as their hobbies, favorite activities, cultural background, personality traits, and talents. Remind them that there are no right or wrong answers; the goal is to create a collage that reflects who they are.

6. Once the children have collected enough images and words, have them arrange their collages on construction paper or poster board. They can use glue or glue sticks to secure the images in place. Encourage them to be creative with arranging and layering images and words to create a visually interesting design.

7. If desired, allow the children to use stickers, masking tape, or other decorative items to embellish their collages.

8. When the collages are complete, allow the children to share their work with the group. Encourage them to discuss the images and words they chose, explaining how they represent their unique qualities and interests.

9. Reflect on the activity, discussing the different interests, talents, and qualities represented in the children's collages. Emphasize the importance of embracing and celebrating our own uniqueness and the uniqueness of others.

The Create a Unique Me Collage activity helps children explore and celebrate their individuality, develop a greater appreciation for their uniqueness, and foster an understanding of the diversity among their peers.

11

Andy's Helping Hand

Responsibility and helping out, teamwork and cooperation, empathy and support, pride in contributing, sharing lessons with others

A mong the hustle and bustle of a busy anthill was a young ant named Andy, who was always eager to explore the world beyond his home. However, when it came to helping out and doing chores, Andy would rather go on an adventure than lend a helping hand.

One sunny day, Andy noticed that his mommy looked tired and overwhelmed as she worked on her never-ending list of chores. He realized she had been doing everything alone and felt guilty for not helping out. "Mommy," Andy said, "you look really tired. Why don't I help you with some of the chores today? We can finish them faster if we work together."

His mommy smiled warmly, grateful for Andy's offer. "Thank you, Andy. That would be wonderful. We all must do our part to maintain our home."

Together, they started by gathering food for the family. As they worked side by side, Andy noticed how quickly they could collect food when they both did their part.

Next, they moved on to tidying up their home. Andy's mommy showed him how to organize the different rooms and explained the importance of keeping their living spaces clean and comfortable for everyone. Andy began to understand how every ant's contribution mattered as they worked.

While they were cleaning, Andy's little sister, Bella, came running into the kitchen. "I accidentally spilled some sugar!" she exclaimed, worried about the mess. Andy's mommy encouraged him to help Bella clean up the sugar, stressing that being there for each other in times of need was important.

Andy and Bella worked together to clean up the mess, and Andy felt a sense of pride in taking responsibility for helping his family. He realized that every task, no matter how small, was crucial in keeping their anthill thriving and harmonious.

Andy's mommy looked much happier and less overwhelmed by the end of the day, thanks to Andy's help. He understood that taking responsibility and helping with chores was essential for their anthill and a way to contribute to his family's well-being.

From that day on, Andy the Ant became a responsible helper at home, always eager to lend a hand and contribute to his family's happiness. The lesson he learned about helping out and responsibility stayed with him, and he shared it with his friends, spreading the importance of teamwork and cooperation throughout the colony.

Andy and his family continued to work together, taking responsibility for their chores and strengthening their home. With each ant in the colony contributing to the greater good, they created a thriving and harmonious community.

Lessons Revealed

Healing metaphor: The metaphor in this story centers around the theme of responsibility and teamwork, as illustrated by the young ant, Andy, learning to contribute to his family and the anthill. The anthill symbolizes a community where everyone has a role to play, and each member's contributions are vital for the greater good.

Teamwork and cooperation: Andy's experience with his family demonstrates the importance of teamwork and cooperation in completing tasks and maintaining a harmonious environment. Children can learn that working together with others can make tasks easier and more efficient.

Responsibility and helping out: The story highlights the importance of taking responsibility and helping out with chores, as it contributes to the well-being of the family or community. Children can learn that every member of a group has a role to play, and everyone's contribution is essential.

Empathy and support: Andy notices his mother's tiredness and offers to help, showing empathy and understanding. Children can learn to recognize when others may need assistance and understand the importance of offering support.

Pride in contributing: As Andy helps his family, he feels a sense of pride in taking responsibility and contributing to their well-being. This can teach children that they can feel good about themselves when they help others and contribute positively to their community.

Sharing lessons with others: Andy shares his lessons about teamwork and responsibility with his friends, spreading these positive values throughout the colony. Children can learn the importance of sharing their experiences and knowledge, fostering a sense of community and mutual support.

Suggested Activities

Teamwork exercise: Organize group activities that require children to work together, such as building a tower with blocks or solving a puzzle. This helps them understand the importance of teamwork and cooperation.

Chore chart: Create a chore chart for children to help with tasks at home or in the classroom. This teaches them responsibility and the value of contributing to their family or community.

Role-playing: Set up role-playing scenarios where children can practice offering help to others and learn how to accept help when needed. This helps develop social skills and empathy.

Story extension: Encourage children to write or draw a continuation of Andy's story, exploring how he and his family continue to work together and help others in the colony. This activity fosters creativity and empathy.

Group discussions: Facilitate group discussions where children can share their thoughts and feelings about helping, teamwork, and responsibility. This allows children to express themselves and learn from others' experiences.

Acts of kindness: Encourage children to perform acts of kindness for others, particularly those struggling or needing assistance. This activity promotes empathy and compassion.

Helping hands craft: Provide materials for children to create their own "helping hands" craft, which they can use to track their acts of service and helpfulness. This activity encourages creativity and reinforces the value of helping others.

Gratitude journal: Encourage children to maintain a gratitude journal where they can write down the things they are grateful for, including times when others have helped them or when they have helped others. This activity helps children develop gratitude and a positive outlook on life.

"Helping Hero" award: Create a "Helping Hero" award to be given to a child who demonstrates exceptional helpfulness and teamwork. This provides positive reinforcement and encourages children to be responsible and helpful.

Problem-solving exercise: Present children with a problem or challenge they must solve together as a team. This helps them understand the importance of cooperation and working together to achieve a common goal.

"Helping Hands Craft" Activity

The Helping Hands Craft activity encourages children to think about ways they can help others and contribute positively to their community. By creating a visual representation of their helping hands, children are reminded of the importance of kindness and their impact on others.

Materials:

- Construction paper
- Scissors
- Pencil or pen
- Markers or colored pencils
- Glue, additional decorative materials (stickers, glitter, etc.)

Instructions:

1. Begin by discussing the concept of helping others and the importance of kindness. Talk about how children can support their families, friends, and community.

2. Introduce the Helping Hands Craft activity. Explain that the purpose of this activity is to create a visual reminder of the different ways they can help others.

3. Provide each child with a piece of construction paper. Encourage them to choose a color that they like or represents kindness to them.

4. Have the children trace both hands onto the construction paper using a pencil or pen. Ensure they leave enough space between the hands to allow cutting them out.

5. Assist the children in cutting out their traced handprints.

6. Once the handprints are cut out, have the children write or draw one way to help others on each finger of their handprints using markers or colored pencils.

7. Encourage them to think of different acts of kindness and ways to support others daily.

8. If desired, allow the children to decorate their helping hands with additional materials, such as stickers or glitter.

9. When the helping hands are complete, allow the children to share their work with the group. Encourage them to discuss the acts of kindness they chose and why those actions are important.

10. Reflect on the activity, discussing the different ways the children have chosen to help others and the impact these actions can have on their community.

11. Display the completed helping hands in a prominent area, such as a bulletin board or classroom wall, as a visual reminder of the importance of kindness and helping others.

The Helping Hands Craft activity helps children explore the concept of kindness, develop an understanding of the impact their actions can have on others, and serves as a visual reminder of the importance of helping others in their daily lives.

12

The River of Truth

Honesty and truthfulness, consequences of deception, maintaining trust, wisdom and guidance from elders, personal growth and commitment to values

A young lion named Leo was born in the heart of the African savannah, where the sun burned brightly, and the tall grass swayed gently in the breeze. From the moment he opened his eyes and gazed out at the endless expanse of his home, Leo was filled with curiosity and a fierce determination to explore the world around him.

One radiant day, Leo stumbled upon a wise elephant named Eldon, known far and wide for his knowledge and grace. The young cub was mesmerized by the ancient elephant's colossal stature, and he approached Eldon to learn about the secrets of life in the savannah.

Sensing the cub's thirst for knowledge, Eldon shared a tale to teach Leo the importance of honesty. He began in a deep, resounding voice, "Leo, my young friend, let me tell you the story of the luminous river of truth."

"In the heart of the savannah, a river flows with waters as clear and radiant as the sky. This river quenches the thirst of the animals who drink from it and their yearning for truth and wisdom."

"The shimmering waters of the river represent the honesty and truthfulness that flow among the creatures of the savannah. When we speak the truth, we maintain the river's luminous clarity, creating harmony and balance in our lives and the world around us."

"But what happens when we deceive or lie, young cub?" Eldon paused, his wise eyes gazing at Leo, who hung onto every word. Eldon continued, "When we lie, we cast dark shadows on the river's surface. The once-clear waters grow dark and murky, making it difficult for others to see the truth. With each lie we tell, the water grows darker."

Leo listened carefully, his heart beating in sync with the rhythm of Eldon's words. The wise elephant pressed on, "When the river is tainted, the harmony and balance of the savannah are disrupted. Animals grow wary of one another, friendships falter, and trust fades like the setting sun."

Leo nodded, grasping the profound story Eldon had shared. The esteemed elephant added, "Remember, young cub, the river of truth is the lifeblood of our existence. By being honest and truthful, we keep the waters clear and bright, allowing trust and harmony to flourish among us."

Embracing Eldon's wisdom, Leo pledged to uphold the values of truthfulness and honesty. As he matured into a powerful and respected lion, he became a symbol of integrity for the animals of the savannah.

The river of truth flowed, pure and radiant, nourishing the lives of all who depended upon it. Leo never wavered in his commitment to maintaining the river's clarity, knowing that a single lie could cast a long shadow and only the truth could illuminate the path to an honest life.

Lessons Revealed

Healing metaphor: The metaphor in "The River of Truth" centers around honesty and its impact on relationships and the community. With its clear and radiant waters, the river symbolizes honesty, trust, and the harmony that exists when individuals are truthful with one another. The darkening of the waters when lies are told, represents the damage that deception can cause to relationships and the overall well-being of a community.

Honesty and truthfulness: The story emphasizes the importance of honesty and truthfulness in maintaining harmonious relationships with others. Children can learn that being truthful and honest is a fundamental aspect of building trust with others and creating a positive environment.

Consequences of deception: The tale illustrates the consequences of deception and dishonesty, showing how lies can create mistrust and discord in a community. Children can learn that lying has negative effects, and it is always better to be honest, even when it seems difficult.

Maintaining trust: Leo's journey emphasizes the importance of maintaining trust among friends and community members. Children can learn the significance of trust and how their actions impact those around them. By upholding the values of truthfulness and honesty, Leo can contribute to the well-being and happiness of the animals.

Wisdom and guidance from elders: The story highlights the importance of seeking wisdom and guidance from elders. Children can learn that elders often possess valuable knowledge and experiences to help them grow and navigate life's challenges.

Personal growth and commitment to values: Leo's development shows the importance of personal growth and commitment to values. Children can learn that embracing and upholding positive values can help them grow into responsible and respected individuals..

Suggested Activities

Story retelling: Encourage children to retell the story in their own words or through drawings.

Role-playing: Set up scenarios where children can practice being honest and truthful, even in challenging situations. This activity helps develop communication skills and moral decision-making.

Honesty discussions: Facilitate group discussions where children can share their experiences with honesty and dishonesty, exploring the consequences of each. This encourages self-reflection and helps children understand the importance of honesty.

Create a "River of Truth" mural: Provide art supplies for children to create a large "River of Truth" mural, representing honesty and its importance in their lives. This activity fosters creativity and teamwork while reinforcing the story's message.

The consequences of dishonesty: Ask children to brainstorm a list of consequences that could arise from dishonesty, either in their lives or in the story's context. This activity helps them understand the potential negative outcomes of lying.

Honesty pledge: Encourage children to pledge to be honest and truthful in their actions and words. This reinforces the importance of honesty and integrity in their daily lives.

Truth and trust activity: Organize an activity or game that highlights the importance of trust and how honesty can build or maintain it. This helps children understand the connection between honesty and trust.

Write an honesty poem or song: Invite children to write a poem or song about honesty and its importance, using the story as inspiration. This activity encourages creativity and self-expression while reinforcing the value of honesty.

"Honesty Hero" award: Create an "Honesty Hero" award to give to a child who demonstrates exceptional honesty and integrity. This provides positive reinforcement and encourages children to be honest and truthful.

Journaling: Encourage children to keep a journal where they can reflect on their experiences with honesty and dishonesty, as well as the lessons they've learned from the story. This activity promotes self-reflection and personal growth.

"River of Truth Mural" Activity

The River of Truth Mural activity encourages children to think about the importance of honesty and truthfulness in their lives. By working together to create a visual representation of a river filled with truthful statements, children will learn the value of honesty and the positive impact it can have on their relationships.

Materials:

- Large roll of white or blue paper (or multiple pieces of construction paper taped together)
- Markers, colored pencils, or crayons
- Optional: stickers, glitter, and other decorative materials

Instructions:

1. Begin by discussing the concept of honesty and the importance of telling the truth. Talk about different situations where honesty is important and how truthfulness can positively impact relationships with family and friends.

2. Introduce the River of Truth Mural activity. Explain that the purpose of this activity is to create a visual representation of a river filled with truthful statements, showing the importance of honesty in their lives.

3. Unroll the large piece of white or blue paper or tape together the pieces of construction paper, creating a long, flowing "river" shape. Lay the paper out on a table or the floor, providing enough space for the children to work on the mural.

4. Invite the children to think of truthful statements about themselves, their experiences, or their feelings. These statements can be simple, such as "I love my family," or complex, like "I feel sad when my friends don't include me."

5. Have the children write or draw their truthful statements on the river paper using markers, colored pencils, or crayons. Encourage them to be creative and use various colors to make their statements stand out.

6. If desired, allow the children to decorate the river with additional materials, such as stickers or glitter, to enhance the visual representation of their truthful statements.

7. When the river is filled with truthful statements, provide an opportunity for the children to share their work with the group. Encourage them to discuss the statements they chose and why they believe honesty is important in those situations.

8. Reflect on the activity, discussing the different truthful statements the children have shared and the impact that honesty can have on their relationships with others.

9. Display the completed River of Truth Mural in a prominent area, such as a bulletin board or classroom wall, as a visual reminder of the importance of honesty and truthfulness in their daily lives.

The River of Truth Mural activity helps children explore the concept of honesty, develop an understanding of the importance of telling the truth, and serve as a visual reminder of the positive impact that honesty can have on their relationships.

13

Taming Ember's Flame

Anger management, self-control, seeking guidance, visualization and mindfulness, personal growth, impact of emotions on others

O nce upon a time, in a faraway kingdom, there was a bustling city filled with vibrant markets, majestic palaces, and enchanting gardens. Guarding the city gates was a young, fiery dragon named Ember. Ember was an impressive creature with bright, glowing scales that shimmered like a warm sunset, and her wings sparkled like the night sky.

Ember was well-loved by all the people in the city, but sometimes, when angry or upset, she would lose control of her temper. Her flames would grow wild and fierce in these moments, causing the citizens to flee in fear.

One fateful day, as Ember soared high above the city, she noticed a hidden courtyard below. Curious, she landed in the yard and discovered a wise old wizard named Aster. Aster had heard of Ember's struggles with her temper and, with a gentle smile, offered to share a magical story with her.

"Deep within the heart of this city lies a secret garden," began Aster. "This garden is filled with beautiful and exotic flowers. Among them is a rare and special flower called Serenity. It is said that Serenity has the power to calm even the wildest storms within one's heart."

Ember listened carefully, her curiosity growing stronger by the minute. Aster continued, "Serenity is unique. It has petals as soft as silk in shades of soothing blue and calming lavender. At its center, a glowing pearl radiates a gentle light that can bring tranquility to all who gaze upon it."

Intrigued, Ember asked Aster how to find this wondrous flower. The wise wizard replied, "To find Serenity, you must embark on a journey within your heart. When you feel your anger rising, close your eyes, and imagine yourself standing in the secret garden. Envision Serenity before you and breathe in its calming scent."

With gratitude, Ember thanked Aster for his wisdom and set off to practice this new technique. The next time she felt her anger flare up, she closed her eyes and imagined herself in the secret garden. She could see the Serenity flower, with its delicate petals and gentle glow. She breathed in the calming scent and felt her anger fade away like a cloud fading in the sky.

Over time, Ember became better at controlling her fiery temper. Whenever she felt angry or upset, she would remember the Serenity flower and the peace it brought her. The people in the city noticed the change in their beloved dragon and rejoiced, for they no longer feared Ember's raging flames.

And so, the story of the magical flower spread far and wide, helping countless people find their inner calm and transforming the lives of all who gazed upon it. The once fearful city became a symbol of peace, all thanks to the extraordinary journey of Ember, the mindful dragon.

Lessons Revealed

Healing metaphor: The metaphor in this story is the Serenity flower, which represents inner peace and emotional balance. The flower's calming scent, soft petals, and gentle glow symbolize the soothing effect of self-control and emotional regulation in one's life. The story teaches that finding Serenity within oneself can lead to personal growth and harmony within a community. In this case, the journey of Ember, the fiery dragon, demonstrates how embracing inner peace can transform not only an individual's life but also the lives of those around them.

Self-control and managing emotions: The story demonstrates the importance of managing emotions, particularly anger. Children can learn from Ember's journey that finding healthy ways to cope with their feelings and avoid hurting others is essential.

Seeking guidance: Ember learns to control her temper after receiving advice from Aster. This emphasizes the importance of seeking guidance from trusted individuals when facing challenges. Children can learn that they do not have to face their problems alone and that asking for help can lead to growth and understanding.

Visualization and mindfulness: The story introduces the concept of visualization and mindfulness. Ember uses the Serenity flower as a focal point to help her calm down and regain control. Children can learn that practicing mindfulness and visualization can help them cope with difficult emotions and situations.

Personal growth: The story highlights the importance of personal growth and self-improvement. Children can learn that they are capable of change and improvement when they put in the effort and dedication.

Impact of emotions on others: Ember's journey demonstrates how one's emotions can affect others. Children can learn that their actions and emotions impact those around them, and it is essential to be mindful of how they express themselves.

Suggested Activities

Story retelling: Encourage children to retell the story in their own words or through drawings. This helps them understand the narrative and reinforces the message of managing emotions and finding inner peace.

Breathing exercises: Teach children simple breathing exercises to calm themselves when they feel angry or upset. This activity helps develop emotional regulation skills.

Emotion charades: Organize a game of charades where children act out different emotions, helping them recognize and understand various feelings.

Create a serenity garden: Provide art supplies for children to create their own "Serenity Garden," representing a safe and calming space they can imagine when they need to find inner peace. This activity fosters creativity and self-expression.

Discussing triggers: Facilitate group discussions where children can share their experiences with anger or frustration, identifying the triggers that cause these emotions. This encourages self-reflection and understanding of one's emotions.

Coping strategies: Help children brainstorm different coping strategies to manage their emotions, such as talking to a trusted adult, engaging in calming activities, or expressing themselves through art or writing.

Role-playing: Set up role-playing scenarios where children can practice using coping strategies to manage their emotions in various situations. This activity helps develop emotional regulation and communication skills.

Create a calming jar: Assist children in making a "calming jar" filled with glitter, water, and coloring. They can shake the jar when upset and watch the glitter settle, helping them focus and calm down.

Emotional expression through art: Invite children to express their emotions through drawing, painting, or other art forms. This activity encourages creativity and emotional expression.

Journaling: Encourage children to keep a journal where they can reflect on their emotions and the techniques they've learned to manage them. This promotes self-reflection and emotional growth.

"Create a Calming Jar" Activity

A calming jar is a simple and effective tool to help children self-regulate and manage strong emotions. In the story "Taming Ember's Flame," children learn about controlling their emotions and understanding their feelings. Creating a calming jar will give children a tangible tool to practice mindfulness and self-soothing techniques.

Materials:

- Clear plastic jar or bottle with a tight-fitting lid
- Water
- Glitter glue or clear glue
- Glitter (various colors and sizes)
- Optional: food coloring or liquid watercolor paint
- Optional: small beads, sequins, or other decorative items
- Optional: hot glue gun or superglue

Instructions:

1. Begin by discussing the importance of self-regulation and managing strong emotions. Explain how a calming jar can help them focus and relax when they feel overwhelmed or upset.

2. Provide each child with a clear plastic jar or bottle with a tight-fitting lid. Make sure the jar is clean and free of any labels.

3. Fill the jar or bottle about halfway with water.

4. Add glitter glue or clear glue to the water. Start with about 1-2 tablespoons of glue and adjust for the desired effect. The amount of glue will determine the speed at which the glitter settles.

5. Have the children choose their favorite colors of glitter to add to their jars. Encourage them to use a mix of different colors and sizes of glitter for a more visually appealing effect.

6. If desired, add a drop or two of food coloring or liquid watercolor paint to give the water a slight tint. Be careful not to add too much, as this may make it difficult to see the glitter.

7. Fill the jar with additional water, leaving about half an inch of space at the top to allow for proper mixing when the jar is shaken.

8. Seal the jar tightly with the lid. For added security, use a hot glue gun or super glue to ensure the lid is securely attached and won't accidentally come off.

9. Invite the children to shake their calming jars and observe the glitter as it swirls around and slowly settles at the bottom. Explain how they can use their calming jars as a tool for self-regulation when they feel overwhelmed or upset by focusing on the swirling glitter and taking slow, deep breaths.

The Create a Calming Jar activity encourages children to practice self-regulation and mindfulness techniques while providing them with a tangible tool to help manage their emotions. It can serve as a reminder of the lessons learned in "Taming Ember's Flame" and help children develop healthy coping strategies for strong emotions.

14

Whisper's Hidden Treasure

Patience, the power of observation, listening skills, seeking wisdom, lasting happiness

O nce upon a time, a quiet little bunny named Whisper lived in a tranquil meadow. Whisper was a small, gentle rabbit with the softest white fur that glistened like the freshly fallen snow.

Whisper loved hopping around the enchanting meadow, exploring its hidden nooks and crannies and listening to the stories the wind would share with her. She felt deeply connected to the meadow, for it was a place where she could be still and let her senses come alive.

One day, she noticed a group of young animals gathered around a bullfrog named Newton. Newton was known throughout the meadow for his incredible knowledge, and the young animals loved listening to his stories.

As Newton began to weave his latest tale, Whisper noticed that some of the animals were growing restless. They fidgeted, talked, and even played games instead of paying attention to the wise bullfrog. Whisper couldn't understand why they weren't listening, for she knew that the words of the wise bullfrog carried the seeds of growth.

Newton paused his story and looked at the young ones with kind eyes. "My dear friends," he said, "I have a challenge for you. In this meadow, there is a hidden treasure. It holds the secret to lasting happiness. The first one to find it will be rewarded beyond measure."

Immediately, the young animals became excited and rushed off searching for the treasure, their hearts pounding with anticipation. Whisper was curious but didn't run off like the others. Instead, she looked at Newton and asked softly, "Where can I find this treasure?"

Newton smiled warmly at the patient bunny and said, "The treasure is hidden in plain sight, my dear. It can only be found by those who pay attention to the world around them. It is like the sun, which illuminates everything it touches, but only those who stop to feel its warmth and absorb its light can truly appreciate its gift."

Whisper nodded and decided to search for the treasure in her own way. She hopped through the meadow, listening to the wind, the rustling leaves, and the songs of the birds. She paid close attention to the vibrant colors of the flowers, the intricate patterns on the butterfly's wings, and the shapes of the clouds above.

Days turned into weeks, and the young animals grew tired and frustrated. They couldn't find the treasure and began to doubt its existence. Whisper, however, remained patient and continued her journey, her heart as light as a feather.

One glorious afternoon, as she sat by a clear stream, she noticed a small, glittering gem nestled among the pebbles. She carefully picked it up and realized she had found the hidden treasure. The stone radiated light and warmth, filling her heart with a joy she had never known before.

Whisper brought the gem back to Newton and showed it to him. The wise bullfrog smiled, his eyes twinkling like the stars, and said, "You found the treasure, my dear, because you understood the importance of patience, listening, and paying attention. This gem symbolizes the wisdom of truly experiencing the world around you."

And as the sun set on the horizon, casting its warm, golden hues across the land, Whisper knew that the true treasure was not the gem she held in her paws but the happiness and wisdom blossoming within her heart.

Lessons Revealed

Healing metaphor: The symbolic element in this story is the hidden treasure, which represents the wisdom and happiness one can gain by truly experiencing and appreciating the world around them. In the story, Whisper discovers the gem by being patient and attentive. At the same time, other young animals fail to find it because they are impatient and restless. The gem symbolizes personal growth, wisdom, and happiness that comes from being present and mindful in our daily lives.

Patience: The story emphasizes the importance of patience in achieving our goals. Unlike the other young animals who rushed in search of the treasure, Whisper takes her time and approaches the challenge with calmness and thoughtfulness. Children can learn that patience is a virtue that leads to better understanding and more meaningful experiences.

The power of observation: Whisper's journey teaches children the value of paying close attention to the world around them. By listening to the wind, observing the colors and patterns of nature, and immersing herself in her surroundings, Whisper discovers the hidden treasure. This lesson encourages children to be present in their environment and to cultivate their observational skills.

Listening: The story highlights the importance of active listening. Whisper learns that the key to finding the treasure is paying attention to the words of the wise bullfrog. Children can learn that by truly listening to others and absorbing their knowledge, they can gain wisdom and insights that will help them.

Seeking wisdom: The story underscores the importance of seeking wisdom and learning from others. Children can learn the value of seeking guidance from wise and knowledgeable individuals. Newton, the wise bullfrog, serves as a mentor figure to Whisper, sharing the secret to finding the hidden treasure.

Lasting happiness: The story conveys that lasting happiness is not found in material possessions, but in the wisdom, experiences, and connections we cultivate throughout our lives. Children can learn that true happiness comes from within and from meaningful connections with others. The true treasure that Whisper discovers is the happiness and wisdom she gains from her journey.

Suggested Activities

Story retelling: Encourage children to retell the story in their own words or through drawings. This helps them understand the narrative and reinforces the message of patience, listening, and paying attention.

Mindfulness exercises: Teach children simple mindfulness exercises to practice being present and paying attention to their surroundings. This activity helps develop focus and self-awareness.

Nature walk: Organize a nature walk where children can explore their environment, paying attention to the sights, sounds, and smells around them. This encourages observation and appreciation of the natural world.

Hidden treasure hunt: Set up a treasure hunt where children search for hidden "gems" throughout a designated area, emphasizing the importance of patience and observation during the activity.

Listening skills: Facilitate group discussions and games that focus on developing listening skills, such as "Telephone," where children pass a whispered message along a line, or "Simon Says," which requires them to pay attention to verbal instructions.

Create a treasure map: Provide art supplies for children to create their own treasure maps, highlighting the importance of observation and attention to detail.

Mindful coloring: Invite children to participate in mindful coloring activities, where they focus on the process of coloring and the present moment rather than the final product. This activity encourages mindfulness and concentration.

Nature collage: Encourage children to collect items from nature, such as leaves, flowers, or rocks, and create a collage or artwork that represents their observations and appreciation of the natural world.

Storytelling circle: Organize a storytelling circle where children take turns sharing stories, emphasizing the importance of listening and paying attention to the speaker.

"Nature Collage" Activity

In the story "Whisper's Hidden Treasure," children discover the value of appreciating the little treasures found in nature. Creating a nature collage allows them to explore the natural world and express their creativity while reflecting on the lessons from the story.

Materials:

- A large piece of paper or poster board
- Scissors
- Glue or glue sticks
- Pencil or pen (optional)
- Natural materials (e.g., leaves, flowers, twigs, seeds, etc.)
- Magazines or printed pictures of nature (optional)

Instructions:

1. Before beginning the activity, go on a nature walk with the children to collect natural materials for their collage. Encourage them to observe their surroundings and gather interesting items such as leaves, flowers, twigs, seeds, or small stones.

2. Once the natural materials have been collected, provide each child with a large piece of paper or poster board. Ask them to think about the story "Whisper's Hidden Treasure" and consider what elements they would like to include in their collage.

3. Encourage the children to arrange their natural materials on the paper or poster board in a way that represents their interpretation of the story. They can create scenes or abstract designs using the materials they collect.

4. If desired, provide magazines or printed pictures of nature for the children to cut out and include in their collages. This can add more variety and depth to their creations.

5. Once the children are satisfied with their arrangements, have them glue the materials onto the paper or poster board, securing them in place.

6. Allow the collages to dry completely before displaying them. Encourage the children to share their creations with the group and discuss how their collages represent the story and the hidden treasures they discovered in nature.

This nature collage activity fosters creativity, mindfulness, and a connection to the natural world, reinforcing the themes presented in "Whisper's Hidden Treasure."

15

Moxie's Mindful Meadow

Attention, hyperactivity, mindfulness, self-regulation, perseverance,
seeking guidance, sharing wisdom

Treetop Academy is a unique school nestled high among the dense, vibrant jungle trees. Animals from around the wilderness gather there to learn, grow, and discover their hidden talents.

One of the students, Moxie the Monkey, was lively and curious. She loved to swing from branch to branch, always eager to explore new places and learn new things. But Moxie struggled to stay focused in class and sometimes felt overwhelmed by her boundless energy.

One day, their teacher Mr. Bright announced a special project for the class. The assignment was to create a presentation about their favorite jungle animal. Moxie was excited but worried about her ability to concentrate on the project.

While taking a break from her studies, Moxie wandered into a serene meadow at the jungle's edge. The meadow was filled with fragrant flowers, rustling grasses, and gentle babbling brooks. The peacefulness of the meadow seemed to soothe Moxie's restless spirit, and she felt a special connection to this place.

As Moxie sat on the soft grass, she noticed a friendly ladybug with vibrant red and black wings resting on a nearby flower. The ladybug introduced herself as Mindy the Mindful Ladybug.

Moxie shared her struggles at Treetop Academy and her concerns about the upcoming project with Mindy. Mindy listened patiently and then shared a secret with Moxie.

"Within this meadow lies the power to balance your energy and bring peace to your mind," said Mindy. "Whenever you feel your energy growing and your thoughts racing, close your eyes and take a deep breath. Imagine yourself sitting in this meadow, surrounded by the calming presence of nature."

Inspired by the wisdom of Mindy, Moxie practiced this technique. As she imagined herself sitting in the peaceful meadow, she felt more focused and in control of her restless mind.

Back at Treetop Academy, Moxie applied her new skills to her project. She chose to present the fascinating life of the wise elephants in the jungle. Her classmates and teacher were impressed by her dedication and focus.

Moxie's friends saw the positive change in her and asked about her secret. Moxie shared her experience with Mindy the Mindful Ladybug and the Mindful Meadow's calming magic.

Moxie had discovered that by embracing the calming energy of the meadow, she could find balance and harmony within herself. By relying on the wisdom of Mindy the Mindful Ladybug, Moxie learned to navigate her world with a newfound focus.

And so, in the heart of the jungle, Moxie continued her journey alongside her friends, knowing that she could always rely on the healing power of the Mindful Meadow to guide her through any challenge she might face.

Lessons Revealed

Healing metaphor: The symbolic element in this story is the Mindful Meadow, which represents a peaceful, calming space that Moxie can turn to when she needs to find focus and balance her energy. The Mindful Meadow helps Moxie cultivate mindfulness and teaches her how to slow down and concentrate on her tasks, ultimately enabling her to succeed at her project and find inner harmony. By relying on the wisdom of Mindy the Mindful Ladybug and the calming magic of the Mindful Meadow, Moxie learns to navigate her world with a newfound focus and shares this knowledge with her friends, showing the power of mindfulness in bringing positive change to one's life.

Mindfulness: The story introduces the concept of mindfulness, encouraging children to be present and focused on their current experiences. Moxie learns to connect with her surroundings in the meadow, which helps her find peace and balance. This lesson can help children manage their thoughts and emotions more effectively.

Self-regulation: Moxie's journey teaches children the importance of self-regulation. By practicing Mindy's technique of imagining herself in the peaceful meadow, Moxie learns to control her restless energy and stay focused on her tasks. This lesson can help children develop essential skills to manage emotions and behaviors.

Perseverance: Moxie's determination to overcome her struggles demonstrates the value of perseverance. Despite her initial worries about the project, Moxie stays committed and works hard to improve her focus. This lesson can inspire children to persevere in the face of challenges and believe in their ability to overcome obstacles.

Seeking guidance: The story emphasizes the importance of seeking guidance and learning from others. Moxie finds a mentor in Mindy the Mindful Ladybug, who shares valuable advice to help Moxie find balance and focus. This lesson encourages children to be open to learning from others and to seek support when needed.

Sharing wisdom: Moxie's Mindful Meadow highlights the importance of sharing wisdom and experiences. After discovering the power of the Mindful Meadow and Mindy's guidance, Moxie shares her newfound knowledge with her friends at Treetop Academy. This lesson teaches children the value of helping others by sharing insights and wisdom.

Suggested Activities

Story retelling: Ask children to retell the story in their own words or through drawings. This helps them understand the narrative and reinforces the message of mindfulness and focus.

Breathing exercises: Teach children simple breathing exercises they can use to practice mindfulness and self-regulation. This activity helps develop focus and emotional control.

Imaginary Mindful Meadow: Encourage children to create their own "Mindful Meadow" through drawing, painting, or collage. This activity promotes creativity and self-expression.

Guided imagery: Lead children through a guided imagery session, helping them imagine a peaceful place like Moxie's Mindful Meadow. This activity encourages relaxation and mindfulness.

Mindfulness journal: Ask children to keep a journal, recording their thoughts and feelings during mindfulness exercises. This activity promotes self-awareness and reflection.

Mindful movement: Organize a group activity that involves mindful movement, such as yoga or tai chi. This encourages focus and awareness of the body and breath.

Mindful listening: Facilitate group discussions or games that focus on developing mindful listening skills, such as "Sound Detective," where children listen to various sounds and identify them.

Create a mindful space: Help children create a quiet, peaceful space in their environment where they can practice mindfulness exercises without interruption.

Share and reflect: Organize a sharing circle where children can discuss their experiences with mindfulness exercises and what they have learned from the story of Moxie's Mindful Meadow.

"Imaginary Mindful Meadow" Activity

In the story "Moxie's Mindful Meadow," Moxie finds peace and serenity in her mindful meadow. This activity invites children to create their own imaginary mindful meadow, a special place to relax and practice mindfulness.

Materials:

- Blank sheets of paper
- Pencils, pens, or markers
- Coloring materials (e.g., colored pencils, crayons, or markers)
- Magazines, printed pictures, or stickers for collage elements

Instructions:

1. Begin by discussing the story "Moxie's Mindful Meadow" with the children. Talk about the concept of a mindful meadow and how Moxie uses it to find peace and calm.

2. Give each child a sheet of paper and ask them to imagine their own mindful meadow. Encourage them to think about what they would see, hear, smell, and feel in their special place.

3. Have the children draw or write about their imaginary mindful meadow on the paper. They can create a detailed scene, a simple sketch, or even a list of descriptive words.

4. Provide coloring materials such as colored pencils, crayons, or markers so the children can bring their mindful meadows to life with color.

5. Optionally, offer magazines, printed pictures, or stickers for the children to use as collage elements in their mindful meadow creations. This can add depth and personalization to their artwork.

6. Once the children have completed their mindful meadow drawings, invite them to share their creations with the group. Encourage them to describe the elements in their meadow and how they imagine themselves feeling while spending time there.

7. Remind the children that they can use their imaginary meadows as a tool for relaxation and mindfulness. Whenever they feel overwhelmed, they can close their eyes and imagine themselves in their special place, taking deep breaths and finding calm.

This Imaginary Mindful Meadow activity encourages creativity, self-expression, and mindfulness practice, reinforcing the themes presented in "Moxie's Mindful Meadow."

16

Saunter's Slow and Steady Quest

Slow learning, embrace your differences, patience and perseverance, appreciating other's strengths, the value of friendship

Deep in the heart of the rainforest, Saunter the sloth lived a quiet life among his many friends - birds, monkeys, and other playful creatures that each called the rainforest home. Saunter was different from his friends as he moved slowly and carefully at his own pace. Although he found keeping up with his swift and nimble friends challenging, Saunter never allowed this to discourage him. From his cozy spot among the trees, he watched his friends play and explore, longing to be a part of the fun.

One beautiful morning, a mysterious tree grew in the forest's center. The tree bore magical fruits, each with a unique power that could transform those who tasted them. Some fruits granted the gift of empathy, allowing one to deeply understand and feel the emotions of others, while other fruits gave the gift of inspiration. All the forest creatures were eager to claim a fruit for themselves.

The magical fruits glimmered temptingly but were protected by a tangle of vines and thorns that made it nearly impossible to reach them. Saunter's friends tried their hardest, but they could not succeed. Despite his doubts, Saunter knew he had to try.

As Saunter made his slow and steady ascent, his movements caught the attention of a wise toucan named Mango. Mango knew that Saunter's careful pace allowed him to observe and learn from the world in ways others couldn't. His unique approach helped him find solutions overlooked by those who rushed.

Mango looked down at Saunter from high above and shouted, "Your slow pace allows you to see things that others often miss. Embrace this, and you will discover that your true power lies within your differences."

Inspired by Mango's words, Saunter continued his journey toward the magical fruit. Along the way, he discovered hidden footholds and paths his friends had overlooked in their haste. Finally, he reached the magical fruit and carefully plucked one from the tree.

When Saunter shared the magical fruit with his friends, they were overjoyed. Each of them gained a special gift, and they realized that Saunter's unique way of learning and doing things had made it all possible. They began to appreciate the value of each other's differences, understanding that everyone had their own pace and unique talents.

Over time, Saunter and his friends became inseparable. They discovered true friendship wasn't just about having fun but embracing their differences and celebrating each other's strengths.

Lessons Revealed

Healing metaphor: The magical tree with its magical fruits is a metaphor for personal growth, transformation, and discovering one's unique talents. The tree represents the challenges and opportunities that life presents, and the fruits symbolize the rewards that come from embracing one's individuality and using their unique strengths to overcome obstacles.

Embrace your differences: Saunter the Sloth teaches children that being different is not a weakness but a strength. His slow and steady approach to reaching the magical fruits allows him to find solutions his friends had overlooked. This lesson encourages children to embrace their uniqueness and understand that their differences can be an asset.

Patience and perseverance: Saunter's journey to the magical fruits demonstrates the value of patience and perseverance. Despite his slow pace and initial doubts, Saunter remains determined to reach his goal. This lesson teaches children the importance of staying committed to their goals, even when the journey is difficult or slow.

Appreciating others' strengths: The story highlights the importance of appreciating the strengths and talents of others. This lesson encourages children to appreciate the unique strengths of their peers and learn from their differences. Saunter's friends learn to recognize and celebrate his unique abilities, leading to a deeper understanding and appreciation of each other.

The value of friendship: Saunter's Slow and Steady Quest emphasizes the importance of true friendship. Saunter and his friends learn that friendship is not just about having fun but about embracing each other's differences and supporting one another. This lesson teaches children the value of building strong, supportive relationships with their peers.

Learning from others: The story illustrates the importance of listening to and learning from others. It encourages children to be open to learning from others and recognizing the wisdom in those around them. Mango, the wise toucan, offers Saunter encouragement and wisdom, helping him see the value in his unique approach.

Suggested Activities

Story retelling: Ask children to retell the story in their own words or through drawings. This can reinforce the message of embracing differences and unique strengths.

Self-reflection: Encourage children to reflect on their own unique strengths, talents, and qualities that make them special. They can write or draw about these traits in a journal or on paper.

Group discussion: Facilitate a group discussion about embracing differences and supporting each other's unique qualities. Encourage children to share examples from their own lives.

Creative writing: Ask children to write a short story or poem about a character who discovers the importance of embracing their differences and unique strengths.

Art activity: Invite children to create a piece of art that represents their unique talents and qualities. They can use a variety of materials, such as paint, clay, or collage.

Role-playing: Organize role-playing activities where children act out scenarios that require understanding and appreciating differences in others, such as Saunter's experience in the rainforest.

Teamwork challenge: Set up a teamwork activity where children must rely on each other's unique strengths and abilities to solve a problem or complete a task.

Celebrate differences: Organize a special day where children can showcase and celebrate their talents, hobbies, and interests.

Share and reflect: Provide opportunities for children to share their artwork, writing, or other projects related to the story and discuss what they have learned about embracing differences and unique strengths.

"Celebrate Differences" Activity

In the story "Saunter's Slow and Steady Quest," Saunter learns the importance of embracing and celebrating his differences. This activity encourages children to recognize and appreciate the unique qualities of their peers.

Materials:

- Blank sheets of paper

- Pencils, pens, or markers
- Coloring materials (e.g., colored pencils, crayons, or markers)

Instructions:

1. Begin by discussing the story "Saunter's Slow and Steady Quest" with the children. Talk about the message of embracing and celebrating the differences that make each individual unique.

2. Give each child a blank sheet of paper and ask them to draw a self-portrait or a picture of themselves. Encourage them to include details that represent their unique qualities, such as their favorite color, hobby, or special talent.

3. Once the children have completed their self-portraits, invite them to share their drawings with the group. Encourage them to describe the unique qualities they included in their portraits.

4. Next, ask the children to pair up with a partner. Have them look at their partner's self-portrait and discuss the unique qualities they see in each other.

5. Provide each child with another blank sheet of paper. Ask them to draw a picture or write a short description of something unique about their partner that they admire or find interesting.

6. Once the children have completed their drawings or descriptions, invite them to share their findings with the group. Encourage them to discuss the unique qualities they discovered in their partners and how this makes their partners special.

7. Conclude the activity by reinforcing the story's message: that we should celebrate the differences in ourselves and others, as they make us unique and valuable.

This Celebrate Differences activity encourages children to recognize and appreciate the unique qualities of their peers, fostering empathy, understanding, and the celebration of diversity. It reinforces the themes in "Saunter's Slow and Steady Quest."

17

Proxy's Online Lesson

Finding balance, the importance of online safety, reconnecting with nature, the value of friendship, embracing the digital world mindfully

A mong the swaying trees and rustling leaves of the Greenleaf Woods, there lived a porcupine named Proxy, who had a mind as sharp as his quills. Proxy was no ordinary porcupine; his quills shimmered with a rainbow of colors, making him a captivating sight to behold.

One sunny day, Proxy stumbled upon a strange device nestled between the roots of an old tree. It was a tablet abandoned by a forgetful traveler. Intrigued by this extraordinary object, Proxy embarked on a thrilling adventure into the digital world. He marveled at the endless wonders of the internet, from hilarious videos and interactive games to engaging forums where he could chat with animals from around the world.

As the days turned into weeks, Proxy spent more and more time with the tablet. He began to notice that his once-radiant quills had started to lose their shine. His energy weakened, and his once-vibrant glow had faded.

Concerned about Proxy, his close and caring friend, Sasha the Skunk, offered some advice. Sasha spoke to Proxy about the importance of finding a balance between the digital world and the natural wonders of the forest. She encouraged Proxy to reconnect with his woodland friends, immerse himself in the forest's beauty, and take breaks from screens to keep his quills radiant and sharp.

Sasha shared important lessons about online safety as they ventured through the forest together. Sasha explained that sharing too much personal information online was akin to scattering his precious quills carelessly, leaving him vulnerable to those who may wish him harm. She compared Proxy's quills to a guardian shield, emphasizing the need for care and caution in the digital world, just as in the forest.

Proxy listened to Sasha's advice and resolved to make a change. He started to limit his screen time, becoming more mindful of his online presence. He protected his personal information, such as his full name, age, and location, just as he guarded his treasured quills.

As Proxy committed to finding a balance between his digital and natural worlds, he turned to Sasha for help in rediscovering the enchanting beauty of Greenleaf Woods. Together, they set out on a series of adventures that would remind Proxy of the joys of staying active and engaged with his surroundings.

Proxy and Sasha delighted in the wonders of their environment, from the joyful songs of the birds to the beautiful patterns found on the forest floor. Each day, Proxy's love for the natural world grew even stronger, and his appreciation for the simple beauty of the outdoors deepened.

As Proxy embraced balance, his quills regained their vibrant glow, and he felt more energetic and engaged with the world around him. With Sasha's guidance, Proxy discovered the joy of combining the digital world into his life while remaining grounded in the gorgeous Greenleaf Woods and the warmth of his cherished friends.

Lessons Revealed

Healing metaphor: Proxy's radiant quills serve as a metaphor for one's mental, emotional, and physical well-being. As Proxy becomes more absorbed in the digital world and neglects the natural environment around him, his quills lose their shine, reflecting the negative impact on his well-being. By finding a balance between the digital and natural worlds, Proxy's quills regain their vibrancy.

Finding balance: The story highlights the importance of balancing screen time and real-life experiences. This lesson can encourage children to find a healthy balance between their digital and real-life experiences.

The importance of online safety: Sasha the Skunk provides Proxy with valuable advice about protecting personal information online, comparing it to guarding his treasured quills. This lesson helps children understand the importance of online safety and the need to be cautious with the information they share online.

Reconnecting with nature: Proxy's journey back into the beauty of Greenleaf Woods reminds children of the wonders of nature and the importance of staying connected to the natural world. The story encourages children to appreciate the outdoors and engage in activities that promote a healthy and active lifestyle.

The value of friendship: Sasha's support and guidance help Proxy regain balance in his life and rediscover the joys of Greenleaf Woods. This lesson teaches children about the value of true friendship and the importance of having someone to lean on when they need help.

Embracing the digital world mindfully: The story also demonstrates that technology can be a valuable tool for learning and connecting with others when used mindfully. Proxy continues to enjoy the digital world, but he does so with a newfound sense of balance and awareness.

Suggested Activities

Story retelling: Have children retell the story in their own words, either verbally or through drawings. This helps them understand the narrative and reinforces the message of balancing the digital and natural worlds.

Digital safety discussion: Facilitate a group discussion about online safety, focusing on the importance of protecting personal information and being mindful of screen time.

Nature exploration: Encourage children to explore their natural environment, observing and appreciating the beauty around them. They can write or draw about their experiences in a journal.

Screen time tracker: Help children create a screen time tracker to monitor and manage their digital usage. Discuss strategies for finding a balance between screen time and outdoor activities.

Creative writing: Ask children to write a short story or poem about a character who learns the importance of finding a balance between the digital world and the natural environment.

Art activity: Invite children to create a piece of art that represents the importance of balancing technology with nature, using various materials such as paint, clay, or collage.

Role-playing: Organize role-playing activities where children act out scenarios related to online safety, digital well-being, and finding a balance between technology and nature.

Teamwork challenge: Set up a teamwork activity where children must work together to solve a problem or complete a task, emphasizing the importance of online and offline communication and collaboration.

Share and reflect: Provide opportunities to share artwork, writing, or other projects related to the story. Discuss what they have learned about balancing their digital and natural worlds.

"Digital Safety Discussion" Activity

In the story "Proxy's Online Lesson," Proxy learns about the importance of online safety and how to navigate the digital world responsibly. This activity facilitates a discussion among children about the importance of digital safety and provides guidelines for staying safe online.

Materials:

- A whiteboard, blackboard, or large sheet of paper
- Markers or chalk

Instructions:

1. Begin by discussing the story "Proxy's Online Lesson" with the children. Talk about Proxy's experience online and the importance of digital safety.

2. Write the following topics on the whiteboard, blackboard, or large sheet of paper:

- Online privacy
- Password security
- Cyberbullying
- Sharing personal information
- Communicating with strangers online
- Appropriate online behavior

3. Divide the children into small groups or pairs and assign one of the above topics to each group. Ask the groups to discuss their topic and develop a list of tips or guidelines for staying safe online related to their assigned topic.

4. After the groups have had time to discuss and create their list, invite them to share their findings with the whole group.

5. As each group shares their tips, write them down on the whiteboard, blackboard, or large sheet of paper under the corresponding topic.

6. Once all the groups have shared, go through the list and discuss the importance of each guideline in ensuring online safety.

7. Conclude the activity by emphasizing the importance of digital safety and encouraging the children to practice these guidelines when using the internet.

The Digital Safety Discussion activity allows children to engage in a meaningful conversation about the importance of online safety. It reinforces the themes presented in "Proxy's Online Lesson" and equips children with practical tips to navigate the digital world safely and responsibly.

18

The Ocean of Possibilities

Learning challenges, dyslexia, resilience and growth, the power of support, perseverance, embracing challenges, celebrating achievements

In the depths of the vast blue ocean stood a school unlike any other – Coral Academy. It was a place where marine creatures from all corners came together to learn and expand their horizons. One of the school's most enthusiastic students was a young dolphin named Finley.

Finley was a bright and curious dolphin, always eager to learn new things. However, he struggled with dyslexia, making reading and understanding written words difficult. This challenge often left him feeling isolated and frustrated, but he was determined to overcome it.

One day, during a lesson on ocean currents, Finley's teacher, Professor Octavius, a brilliant and kind-hearted octopus, decided to illustrate the topic with a healing story. He told the students about a beautiful and unique coral reef that thrived within the ocean's depths.

"This coral reef is like each of our lives," Professor Octavius said, waving his tentacles gracefully. "Though its beauty is forged through the trials of time and the pressures of the ocean, it stands as a testament to resilience and growth."

As the students listened, Finley's eyes widened with curiosity. He had never considered his struggle in such a positive light. Maybe, he thought, he too could find resilience and growth within himself, just like the coral reef.

Determined to grow stronger, Finley sought help from his friends and teachers. He attended extra tutoring sessions with Professor

Octavius, who shared various techniques and tools to help Finley understand the written word. He practiced reading with his best friend, Shelly, a sea turtle, who was always patient and encouraging.

With time and perseverance, Finley's reading abilities started to improve. Though the words swirled and danced on the pages, he was no longer overwhelmed by them. Instead, he learned to embrace the challenges, allowing them to shape and strengthen him like the resilient coral reef.

One day, as the school year was ending, Professor Octavius assigned the class a final project – a presentation on a marine creature of their choice. Finley decided to research and present on the humpback whale, a majestic creature that fascinated him. With Shelly's help, he spent many hours studying and preparing, determined to make his presentation the best it could be.

When the day of the presentation arrived, Finley's heart pounded in his chest as he stood in front of the class. He took a big deep breath and began, feeling his confidence growing. His classmates listened in awe as he spoke, captivated by the depth of his knowledge and passion.

When Finley finished his presentation, the room erupted in applause. The young dolphin had found healing, overcoming the challenges with the help of those around him. His friends and teachers beamed with pride, and even Finley couldn't help but smile, knowing how far he had come.

From that day on, Finley continued to thrive at Coral Academy, growing stronger and more resilient each day. The once-daunting waves of his dyslexia had transformed into a source of growth and strength, and the young dolphin swam onward, eager to explore the vast ocean of possibilities before him.

Lessons Revealed

Healing metaphor: The coral reef, described as growing and thriving despite the trials of time and pressures of the ocean, serves as a metaphor for resilience and personal growth in the face of challenges. In the story, Finley, who struggles with dyslexia, learns to embrace his difficulties, drawing strength and growth from them, much like the coral reef. The ocean of possibilities mentioned at the end of the story is also a metaphor, representing the vast potential and opportunities available to Finley as he continues to overcome his challenges and grow as a person.

Resilience and growth: The story emphasizes the importance of resilience and growth through the metaphor of the coral reef. Just like the coral reef that thrives in challenging conditions, Finley learns to embrace his dyslexia and grow stronger from it. This lesson encourages children to approach their challenges with a positive mindset and learn from them.

The power of support: Finley's journey is made possible by the support and guidance he receives from his friends and teachers. Professor Octavius and Shelly play a vital role in helping Finley overcome his dyslexia by offering patience, encouragement, and useful techniques. This lesson teaches children the value of seeking help and support when they face challenges.

Perseverance: Finley demonstrates perseverance by attending extra tutoring sessions and practicing reading with Shelly. His dedication to overcoming his dyslexia shows children the importance of not giving up when faced with difficulties and that hard work and determination can lead to success.

Embracing challenges: The story encourages children to embrace challenges and view them as opportunities for growth. Finley's journey reminds us that challenges can shape and strengthen us, just like the coral reef in Professor Octavius's story.

Celebrating achievements: Finley's success during his presentation is a triumphant moment that highlights the importance of celebrating achievements, no matter how big or small. The pride and joy that Finley and those around him feel show children that their efforts and progress should be acknowledged and appreciated.

Suggested Activities

Story retelling: Have children retell the story of Finley in their own words or through drawings to reinforce the message of resilience, growth, and overcoming challenges.

Personal challenges discussion: Facilitate a group discussion about personal challenges children face and brainstorm strategies for overcoming them.

Resilient coral reef: Discuss the metaphor of the coral reef in the story and how it represents resilience and growth. Encourage children to create artwork or craft projects depicting their "coral reef" of resilience.

Reading buddies: Pair children together to practice reading aloud and offer support to one another, fostering a sense of camaraderie and empathy.

Role models: Encourage children to research and share stories about famous individuals who have overcome challenges, emphasizing the importance of perseverance and resilience.

Goal setting: Help children set realistic goals related to personal challenges, and discuss steps they can take to achieve these goals.

Role-playing: Organize role-playing activities where children act out scenarios related to overcoming challenges and supporting friends who are facing difficulties.

Encouraging words: Have children create a list of encouraging phrases to support themselves and others when facing challenges.

Share and reflect: Provide opportunities for children to share their artwork, stories, or other projects related to the story and discuss what they have learned about overcoming challenges.

Read aloud: Read other stories or books that focus on the themes of resilience, growth, and overcoming personal challenges.

"Resilient Coral Reef" Activity

In the story "Ocean of Possibilities," a young dolphin named Finley learns about resilience and the importance of overcoming challenges. This activity allows children to create their own resilient coral reef, symbolizing the strength and adaptability of individuals and communities in the face of adversity.

Materials:

- Construction paper or card stock (various colors)
- Scissors
- Glue sticks or liquid glue
- Markers, crayons, or colored pencils
- Large sheet of blue paper or poster board
- Optional: stickers, sequins, or other decorative items

Instructions:

1. Begin by discussing the story "Ocean of Possibilities" with the children. Talk about Finley's journey and the lessons he learned about resilience and overcoming challenges.

2. Tell the children that they will create a coral reef together, representing their strength and ability to adapt to challenges.

3. Give each child a few sheets of colored construction paper or card stock. Ask them to draw and cut out various shapes of coral,

fish, and other sea creatures that live in the coral reef. Encourage them to be creative and think about the unique characteristics of each sea creature.

4. Provide the children markers, crayons, or colored pencils to decorate and add details to their coral, fish, and sea creatures.

5. Once the children have completed their coral, fish, and sea creatures, gather them together and arrange them on a large sheet of blue paper or poster board to create the coral reef scene.

6. As the children attach their creations to the blue paper or poster board with glue, encourage them to discuss how their coral, fish, and sea creatures represent resilience and the ability to overcome challenges.

7. Once the resilient coral reef is complete, display it in a prominent location as a reminder of the lessons learned and the importance of resilience in the face of adversity.

The Resilient Coral Reef activity reinforces the themes of resilience and adaptability found in the story "Ocean of Possibilities." By working together to create a vibrant coral reef, children are reminded of their own strength and ability to overcome challenges.

19

The Gift of Knowledge

The value of education, empathy, friendship, sharing knowledge, confidence and self-esteem, making a positive impact

Once upon a time, a young owl named Ollie lived in the heart of a dense, emerald-green forest. In this forest, owls were revered as the wisest creatures, and those with the most knowledge were held in the highest esteem.

One day, Ollie's father gathered Ollie and his siblings for a lesson. He told them, "My little owlets, always remember that learning is like the wind beneath your wings. It lifts you, so you can soar to great heights and see the world in ways you never imagined."

Ollie took his father's words to heart and dedicated himself to learning as much as possible. As he learned, he began to see the forest from a different perspective. He studied the stars above, the plants below, and the creatures around him.

One day, as Ollie was reading under the shade of a great oak tree, he noticed a group of birds teasing a young flying squirrel. Ollie, who had just learned about empathy, approached the squirrel. The squirrel, embarrassed and sad, ran away to hide in a bush.

"Hey there, my name is Ollie," he said softly, trying not to startle the young squirrel. "I saw what happened and wanted to see if you were okay."

The squirrel peeked out from behind the leaves, wiping tears from his eyes. "I'm Chip," he replied. "I'm just so tired of being made

fun of. The other animals say I'm not smart because I don't know as much as they do."

Ollie, who understood the value of education, decided to help Chip. He offered to teach Chip everything he knew about the forest and its inhabitants. Chip, grateful for Ollie's kindness, eagerly accepted the offer.

Over the next few weeks, Ollie and Chip spent their days learning and exploring together. Ollie taught Chip about the plants and their uses, the stars and their stories, and the animals and their habits. Chip, in turn, taught Ollie about the secret pathways and how to find the tastiest fruits, nuts, and berries in the forest.

As Chip's knowledge grew, so did his confidence. The other animals noticed the change and treated him with newfound respect. Chip realized that the wind beneath his wings had been there all along; he just needed someone to help him harness it.

Ollie, too, gained from experience. He discovered that sharing his knowledge helped others and enriched his understanding of the world. He realized that education was important, but using that knowledge to help others and make the world a better place was just as important.

And so, Ollie and Chip continued learning and growing together, soaring higher and higher on the wings of knowledge. They symbolized hope and wisdom in the forest, inspiring others to seek and share knowledge with those around them. The wind carried them to great heights, and they knew that together, they could conquer any challenge that came their way.

Lessons Revealed

Healing metaphor: The wind beneath the wings, which lifts and enables one to soar to great heights, is a metaphor for knowledge and learning. This metaphor emphasizes the transformative power of education and its role in personal growth and empowerment. In the story, Ollie the owl teaches Chip the squirrel about the forest, helping Chip gain confidence and respect from others. By sharing his knowledge, Ollie also gains a deeper understanding of the world and the importance of using knowledge to help others.

The value of education: Ollie's father emphasizes the importance of learning and how it can lift individuals to great heights. This lesson teaches children to appreciate education and seek knowledge to grow and achieve their dreams.

Empathy: Ollie demonstrates empathy when he approaches Chip, who the other animals are teasing. By showing compassion and understanding, Ollie can forge a strong bond with Chip, reminding children of the importance of being empathetic towards others.

Friendship: The story highlights the power of friendship and how it can enrich lives. As Ollie and Chip share their knowledge and experiences, they form a strong bond and help each other grow. This lesson encourages children to seek meaningful friendships and learn from one another.

Sharing knowledge: Ollie's decision to share his knowledge with Chip illustrates the power of spreading wisdom and helping others. This lesson encourages children to share their own knowledge and skills with those around them, creating a supportive and collaborative community.

Confidence and self-esteem: As Chip gains knowledge, he also gains confidence and earns the respect of the other animals. This lesson teaches children that learning and self-improvement can positively impact their self-esteem and how others perceive them.

Making a positive impact: Ollie and Chip's journey shows how knowledge and empathy can inspire others and create a positive change in their community. Children can learn that by using their knowledge to help others, they can make the world a better place.

Suggested Activities

Story retelling: Have children retell the story of Ollie and Chip in their own words or through drawings to reinforce the importance of learning and sharing knowledge.

Empathy discussion: Facilitate a group discussion about empathy and the importance of understanding and respecting others' feelings, using the story as a starting point.

Knowledge tree: Encourage children to create a "knowledge tree" with branches representing various topics they are interested in or want to learn more about.

Pair and share: Pair children together to teach each other something new, fostering cooperation, communication, and the sharing of knowledge.

Nature walk: Organize a nature walk where children can explore their surroundings and learn about the local flora and fauna.

Confidence-building activities: Plan activities and games that help build children's confidence and self-esteem, such as team-building exercises or public speaking practice.

Journaling: Encourage children to keep a learning journal where they can record new facts or ideas they discover.

Acts of kindness: Have children brainstorm and perform acts of kindness to help others, emphasizing the importance of using their knowledge for good.

"The Knowledge Tree" Activity

In the story "The Gift of Knowledge," an owl named Oliver shares his wisdom with the other animals in the forest. This activity encourages children to create their own knowledge tree, representing the various lessons and wisdom they've gained in their lives.

Materials:

- Large sheet of paper or poster board
- Construction paper or card stock (various colors)
- Scissors
- Glue sticks or liquid glue
- Markers, crayons, or colored pencils
- Optional: stickers, sequins, or other decorative items

Instructions:

1. Begin by discussing the story "The Gift of Knowledge" with the children. Talk about the wisdom that Ollie the owl shared with the other animals in the forest and how he encouraged them to share their own knowledge.

2. Tell the children that they will create a knowledge tree together, representing the lessons and wisdom they've gained.

3. Draw a large tree trunk and branches with markers or crayons on a large sheet of paper or poster board. Leave plenty of space for the children to add their leaves of knowledge.

4. Give each child a few sheets of colored construction paper or card stock. Ask them to draw and cut out leaf shapes.

5. Provide the children with markers, crayons, or colored pencils to write or draw something they've learned or a piece of wisdom they want to share on their leaves. This could be a lesson from school, a family member, or a personal experience.

6. Optional: Offer stickers, sequins, or other decorative items for children to add to their leaves.

7. Once the children have completed their leaves of knowledge, gather them and have each child share what they wrote or drew on their leaf.

8. After each child has shared their leaf, ask them to glue their leaves onto the tree branches, creating a beautiful and colorful knowledge tree.

9. Display the completed knowledge tree in a prominent location as a reminder of the wisdom and lessons each child has gained and shared with the group.

The Knowledge Tree activity reinforces the themes of sharing knowledge and learning from one another found in the story "The Gift of Knowledge." By working together to create a vibrant knowledge tree, children are reminded of the importance of learning from and sharing wisdom with others.

20

Squeaky's Sleep Solution

Habit control, bedwetting, friendship, determination, the power of a caring community, overcoming challenges

O nce upon a time, a young squirrel named Squeaky lived with his loving family in the heart of a dense green forest. Their cozy treehouse was tucked within the strong branches of a wise old oak tree.

Squeaky loved his treehouse, and every night, he would snuggle up in his soft, comfortable bed made from the most delicate leaves the forest had to offer. As the sun set and the forest grew quiet, Squeaky drifted off to sleep, dreaming about the exciting adventures that awaited him.

One night, the wise old oak tree noticed that Squeaky was having trouble sleeping. A tiny storm cloud would appear in his dreams, causing a gentle rain to fall on his bed, making it damp, cold, and uncomfortable.

The wise old oak tree, who had seen many generations of squirrels come and go, decided it was time to teach Squeaky a valuable lesson. As the first light of day awakened the forest, the old oak tree whispered a secret to Squeaky.

"Squeaky, my dear friend," the tree said in a deep, gentle voice. "I see a tiny storm cloud troubling you during your sleep. It's time to learn an ancient secret of the forest to help you sleep through the night, dry and warm."

Squeaky's eyes sparkled with curiosity, eager to learn the secret. The old oak tree continued, "Within this forest is a magical fruit

called the Dreamberry. It's known to help young squirrels like you find dry, peaceful sleep. To discover it, you must follow the path of the setting sun and seek out the tallest tree in the woods."

Determined to find the Dreamberry, Squeaky gathered his friends - a clever fox, a fearless rabbit, and a mighty beaver - and set off on their journey. As they followed the path of the setting sun, they encountered many challenges that tested their friendship and teamwork, but they never wavered.

Finally, after a long day of adventure and discovery, Squeaky and his friends arrived at the tallest tree in the heart of the woods. There, growing at the base of the majestic tree, they found the magical Dreamberry plant. Its leaves sparkled, and its scent filled the air with a soothing aroma. Carefully, Squeaky picked a few berries and placed them in his bag, excited to return the magical fruit to his treehouse.

Upon returning to his cozy bed, Squeaky thanked the wise old oak tree and shared the Dreamberries with his friends. Together, they prepared a cup of Dreamberry tea. As they slowly sipped the magical drink, they felt a sense of calm and tranquility.

That night, as Squeaky closed his eyes and drifted off to sleep, the tiny storm cloud that once troubled him vanished, replaced by a beautiful, clear night sky filled with twinkling stars.

From that night on, Squeaky slept peacefully, and the bed he loved so much remained warm and dry. Every morning, he would wake up, greeted by the sunrise, symbolizing the warmth and dryness that awaited him.

Lessons Revealed

Healing metaphor: The story centers around Squeaky, a young squirrel who seeks out the magical Dreamberry to resolve his issue of bedwetting. The story can be seen as an allegory for overcoming personal challenges and the importance of friendship and teamwork.

The Dreamberry and the journey to find it represent the efforts and support needed to face and resolve difficulties in life.

Friendship: The bond between Squeaky and his friends is a central theme of the story. Together, they embark on a journey to find the magical Dreamberries, helping each other overcome challenges. This lesson emphasizes the importance of forming strong friendships and supporting one another during difficult times.

Determination: Squeaky's determination to find the Dreamberries demonstrates the power of perseverance. By remaining committed to his goal, Squeaky ultimately succeeds in his quest. This lesson teaches children to stay focused and determined, even when faced with obstacles.

The power of a caring community: The wise old oak tree plays a vital role in Squeaky's journey, sharing its knowledge and guiding him on his quest. The tree's wisdom and support exemplify the importance of a caring community that nurtures and helps its members grow. This lesson encourages children to appreciate and seek out the guidance of others.

Overcoming challenges: Squeaky and his friends encounter various challenges during their journey, but they never give up. By working together and using their unique skills, they overcome each obstacle. This lesson teaches children the importance of resilience and problem-solving, as well as the value of teamwork.

Suggested Activities

Story retelling: Have children retell the story of Squeaky and the Dreamberry in their own words or through drawings to reinforce the message of friendship, teamwork, and overcoming challenges.

Teamwork discussion: Facilitate a group discussion about the importance of teamwork and how Squeaky's friends helped him on his journey to find the Dreamberry.

Create your own magical fruit: Encourage children to use their imagination and create their own magical fruit, complete with a name, appearance, and special abilities.

Acts of friendship: Have children brainstorm and perform acts of friendship to help others, emphasizing the importance of working together and supporting one another.

Dream journal: Encourage children to keep a dream journal where they can record their dreams and reflect on the experiences and emotions they encounter while sleeping.

Nature walk: Organize a nature walk, allowing children to explore their surroundings and learn about the local flora and fauna.

Problem-solving activities: Plan activities and games that help children develop problem-solving skills, such as puzzles, riddles, or scavenger hunts.

Read aloud: Read other stories or books focusing on friendship, teamwork, and overcoming challenges.

Creative writing: Have children write their own adventure story featuring Squeaky and his friends, incorporating the lessons they learned from the Dreamberry story.

Art project: Encourage children to create a visual representation of the magical Dreamberry, using various art supplies and techniques.

"Dream Journal" Activity

In the story "Squeaky's Sleep Solution," Squeaky the squirrel learns the importance of self-control and the power of dreams. This activity encourages children to create dream journals, allowing them to record and explore their dreams.

Materials:

• Blank notebooks or journals (one for each child)

- Markers, crayons, or colored pencils
- Stickers, masking tape, or other decorative items
- Pens or pencils for writing

Instructions:

1. Begin by discussing the story "Squeaky's Sleep Solution" with the children. Talk about Squeaky's journey and the role dreams play in our lives.

2. Tell the children they will create their own dream journal to record and explore their dreams. Explain that a dream journal can help them remember and understand their dreams better.

3. Provide each child with a blank notebook or journal. They can draw pictures, write their name, or create a design that represents them. Encourage them to personalize the cover of their journal using markers, crayons, or colored pencils.

4. Offer stickers, masking tape, or other decorative items for children to further customize their dream journals.

5. Once the children have decorated their journals, discuss the purpose of a dream journal and how to use it. Explain that they should write or draw their dreams as soon as they wake up, as this is when their memories of the dream are the freshest.

6. Provide pens or pencils for the children to write in their journals. Encourage them to write or draw about any dreams they can remember from recent nights. If they can't remember a specific dream, they can write about how they felt when they woke up or any images or emotions that come to mind.

7. Regularly encourage the children to use their dream journals and share their dreams with the group if they feel comfortable doing so. This sharing can promote discussions about common themes in dreams and help children better understand the role dreams play in their lives.

The Dream Journal activity reinforces the themes of sleep and dreams found in the story "Squeaky's Sleep Solution." By creating and using a dream journal, children can better understand and appreciate the power and significance of their dreams.

21

Cally's Courageous Change

Habit control, thumb sucking, embracing change, overcoming fear, believing in oneself, the beauty of transformation

A curious caterpillar named Cally made her home among a fragrant sea of blooming flowers. One sunny day, Cally noticed that all her caterpillar friends were starting to change. They were weaving silky cocoons around themselves, preparing for a magical transformation

Cally was curious and slightly worried, but her mother assured her, "Do not fear, my dear. You, too, shall soon embark on a miraculous journey."

Cally noticed that her friends had an unusual habit. They would gently rub their tiny legs together, creating a beautiful, soothing melody that seemed to give them strength and peace. Intrigued, Cally tried to join in but struggled to find the rhythm. Instead, she would suck on her little front legs, finding comfort in the familiar sensation.

Days passed, and Cally watched in awe as her friends emerged from their cocoons as magnificent butterflies. They had wings in vibrant colors and patterns that danced gracefully in the wind. She longed to join them, to soar high in the sky and feel the sunlight on her wings. But her cocoon remained stubbornly unwoven.

One day, her mother approached Cally and said, "My darling, you have a choice. You can continue to find comfort in your familiar ways or embrace the change that awaits you. The power to transform lies within you."

Cally thought long and hard about her mother's wise words. She realized she needed to welcome the unknown to grow and transform like her friends.

With newfound determination, Cally decided to let go of her old habits. She focused on rubbing her front legs together like her friends, feeling a sense of peace and inner strength.

Feeling ready to embark on her magical journey, Cally slowly weaved a cocoon around herself. The soft and silky threads created a snug blanket around her. As she settled into her cocoon, she felt protected, as if she were cradled by her mother's loving embrace.

After a long, cozy rest, Cally emerged from her cocoon as a breathtaking butterfly with shimmering wings of sapphire blue and glistening gold.

She soared through the sky, feeling the sun's warmth on her wings and the wind's gentle caress. She was grateful to her mother for helping her see the power within her and teaching her the importance of embracing change.

With a heart full of gratitude, Cally vowed to share her story with other young caterpillars, inspiring them to find the strength to transform and discover their true potential.

Lessons Revealed

Healing metaphor: Cally's journey from a caterpillar to a butterfly serves as a metaphor for personal growth, change, and transformation. Just as Cally has to let go of her old habits and embrace the unknown to become a butterfly, people often need to step out of their comfort zones and face challenges to grow and reach their full potential. The process of weaving a cocoon and emerging as a butterfly symbolizes the courage and determination required to undergo significant life changes.

Embracing change: Change is a natural part of life, and Cally's journey teaches children that embracing change can lead to growth and transformation. By welcoming new experiences, children can learn to adapt and thrive in different situations.

Overcoming fear: Cally's initial fear of change is a relatable feeling for many children. The story demonstrates that it is possible to achieve incredible things by facing one's fears and stepping out of one's comfort zone.

Believing in oneself: Cally's transformation into a butterfly is a testament to the power of self-belief. By trusting in her own abilities and making a conscious choice to change, Cally discovers her true potential. This lesson teaches children the importance of having confidence in themselves and their abilities.

The power of support: Cally's mother plays a crucial role in her journey, providing reassurance and guidance. The story emphasizes the importance of a caring community and its positive impact on personal growth.

The value of sharing experiences: Cally's decision to share her story with other young caterpillars highlights the importance of sharing experiences and knowledge with others. By doing so, children can inspire and empower their peers, creating a supportive and compassionate community.

The beauty of transformation: Cally's metamorphosis into a beautiful butterfly is a powerful metaphor for personal growth and transformation. This imagery can help children recognize that they can evolve and reach their full potential with determination.

Suggested Activities

Story retelling: Encourage children to retell the story of Cally in their own words or through drawings, emphasizing the importance of embracing change and personal growth.

Change discussion: Facilitate a group discussion about change and how it can be both scary and exciting. Encourage children to share their personal experiences with change.

Create your own butterfly: Provide art materials for children to create their own butterfly, complete with unique colors and patterns. Encourage them to share the meaning behind their butterfly's design.

Life cycle of a butterfly: Teach children about the life cycle of a butterfly, from egg to caterpillar, cocoon, and finally, butterfly. Discuss the importance of each stage in the process.

Change journal: Encourage children to keep a change journal where they can record and reflect on their personal growth and experiences with change.

Role play: Organize a role-play activity where children can act out the story of Cally's Courageous Change, taking on the roles of Cally, her mother, and her friends.

Growth mindset: Discuss the concept of a growth mindset with children, emphasizing the importance of embracing challenges and learning from mistakes.

Read aloud: Read other stories or books that focus on the themes of change, growth, and self-discovery.

Creative writing: Encourage children to write their own story about a character who goes through a significant change, incorporating the lessons they learned from Cally's story.

Encouragement cards: Have children create encouragement cards for their friends or classmates, featuring words of support and motivation for embracing change and personal growth.

"Create Your Own Butterfly" Activity

In the story "Cally's Courageous Change," Cally undergoes a beautiful transformation into a butterfly, symbolizing the power of change and personal growth. This activity allows children to create their own butterflies, expressing their individuality and creativity.

Materials:

- Construction paper or card stock in various colors
- Scissors
- Glue or glue sticks
- Markers, crayons, or colored pencils
- Pipe cleaners (optional)
- Decorative items such as stickers, sequins, or glitter (optional)

Instructions:

1. Begin by discussing the story "Cally's Courageous Change" with the children. Talk about Cally's transformation into a butterfly and the importance of embracing change and personal growth.

2. Tell the children they will create their own butterflies to represent their uniqueness and creativity.

3. Provide each child with construction paper or card stock in various colors. Encourage them to choose two colors: one for the butterfly's body and one for its wings.

4. For the butterfly's body, have the children cut out a long, thin oval shape from their chosen color.

5. For the wings, instruct the children to fold their chosen construction paper or card stock color in half. While the paper is folded, have them draw half of a butterfly wing shape along the folded edge. Once they cut out the shape and unfold the paper, they will have symmetrical butterfly wings.

6. Have the children glue the butterfly's body onto the center of the wings.

7. Provide markers, crayons, or colored pencils for the children to decorate their butterflies. Encourage them to create unique patterns and designs on the wings, representing their individuality.

8. If using pipe cleaners, have the children cut a small piece and fold it in half to create antennae. They can then glue the antennae to the top of the butterfly's body.

9. If using googly eyes, have the children glue them onto the butterfly's body to create a face.

10. Offer additional decorative items such as stickers, sequins, or glitter for the children to personalize their butterflies further.

11. Once the butterflies are complete, encourage the children to share their creations with the group. Discuss the unique patterns and designs they chose and how each butterfly represents their individuality.

The Create Your Own Butterfly activity reinforces the themes of change, growth, and individuality found in the story "Cally's Courageous Change." Children can express their creativity and celebrate their uniqueness by creating and decorating their butterflies.

22

The Four Food Fairies

Overcoming picky eating habits, the importance of a balanced diet,
encouraging variety in food choices, imagination during mealtime

A family of Four Food Fairies lived deep within the heart of a bustling urban park, hidden away among the trees. Each fairy had a unique gift, and together, they ensured that all children enjoyed their meals and discovered the magic of food.

The first fairy, Nourish, had the power to fill food with essential vitamins and minerals, helping children grow strong and healthy. The second fairy, Flavor, could make any dish taste delightful and delicious. The third fairy, Aroma, could create tantalizing scents that filled the air, beckoning children to their meals. The fourth fairy, Variety, could change a meal's shape, color, and texture, making every mealtime an exciting and enchanting adventure.

One sunny day, the Four Food Fairies came across a little boy named Timmy, known to be very fussy about his meals. Timmy often refused to eat, claiming that his food was too bland, too smelly, or too icky. Hearing this, the Food Fairies knew they had found their next mission: to help Timmy appreciate the wonders of food and teach him to enjoy every bite.

As evening approached, the fairies gathered around Timmy's house, patiently waiting for the perfect moment to work their magic. When Timmy's mother placed the meal on his plate, the fairies sprang into action.

Nourish waved her wand over the vegetables, ensuring they were full of vitamins and minerals. The carrots glowed with bright orange

energy, while the broccoli became a lush, green forest. With a gentle flutter of her wings, Aroma filled the air with the most delightful scents, making Timmy's nose tingle with anticipation. Flavor tapped her wand on the chicken, making it succulent and tender, with a taste so delicious that even the pickiest eater would find it irresistible.

Lastly, Variety used her power to transform the food into an enchanting landscape. The rice turned into soft, fluffy clouds floating above a magical forest of broccoli trees. The carrots transformed into a fleet of vibrant orange sailboats, gliding gracefully on a sea of savory gravy. The chicken morphed into golden, tasty nuggets filled with delight.

Timmy stared in awe at the captivating scene before him. He couldn't resist exploring this magical world with his fork. A symphony of flavors, aromas, and textures filled his senses as he took his first bite. Timmy marveled at the wonders of the food and began to enjoy every mouthful.

Timmy eagerly anticipated every meal from that day on, knowing that the Four Food Fairies were there to guide him on a mouthwatering journey. He learned to appreciate the beauty and importance of his food as he grew strong and healthy.

And so, the Four Food Fairies continued to watch over Timmy, helping him embrace the magic of food and ensuring that he never missed out on the flavorful and nourishing meals that would allow him to grow and thrive.

Lessons Revealed

Healing metaphor: The Four Food Fairies represent the various aspects of food that are important for a balanced and enjoyable meal. Nourish represents nutritional value, Flavor symbolizes taste, Aroma stands for the enticing smells of food, and Variety represents the diverse and exciting nature of food.

Importance of a balanced diet: The story highlights the role of Nourish, the fairy responsible for ensuring that children's food is rich in vitamins and minerals. This lesson teaches children the significance of consuming a balanced diet to maintain their overall health and well-being.

The joy of taste and aroma: Flavor and Aroma, two of the Food Fairies, emphasize the importance of taste and smell in making food enjoyable. This encourages children to explore and appreciate different foods' various flavors and aromas.

Encouraging variety: Variety teaches children the value of experimenting with different types of food. This helps children understand that variety can make mealtimes enjoyable and exciting.

Using imagination during mealtimes: The fairies use their magic to transform Timmy's meal into an enchanting landscape, capturing his imagination and making him excited to eat. This lesson inspires children to use their creativity and imagination during mealtimes, making it a fun and engaging experience.

Overcoming picky habits: Timmy's journey demonstrates that even picky eaters can learn to enjoy various foods. This story can help children struggling with picky eating habits understand the importance of giving different foods a chance and appreciating their taste, aroma, and nutritional value.

The power of teamwork: The fairies work together to help Timmy appreciate his food, showing that teamwork can lead to success. This lesson teaches children the value of collaboration and cooperation in achieving a common goal.

Suggested Activities

Story retelling: Encourage children to retell the story of The Four Food Fairies in their own words or through drawings, emphasizing the importance of eating a variety of healthy foods.

Create your own Food Fairy: Provide art materials for children to create their own food fairy, complete with unique powers related to food and nutrition. Encourage them to share the story behind their fairy's powers.

Healthy eating discussion: Facilitate a group discussion about the importance of eating a balanced diet and trying new foods. Encourage children to share their favorite healthy meals and snacks.

Magical mealtime: Organize a magical mealtime activity where children can use their imaginations to transform their food into an enchanting landscape. Encourage them to describe their imaginary food world to their friends.

Taste test: Host a taste test with various fruits, vegetables, and other healthy foods. Encourage children to describe the flavors, textures, and scents they experience.

Food collage: Have children create a food collage using pictures from magazines or drawings of their favorite healthy foods.

Nutrition lesson: Teach children about the different food groups and importance of incorporating various foods into their diet.

Read aloud: Read other stories or books that focus on the themes of healthy eating, appreciation of food, and imagination.

Creative writing: Encourage children to write their own story about a character who learns to appreciate the wonders of food and the importance of a balanced diet.

Cooking activity: Organize a cooking activity where children can help prepare a healthy meal or snack, emphasizing the importance of trying new foods and enjoying a variety of flavors, textures, and colors.

"Taste Test" Activity

In the story "The Four Food Fairies," the fairies introduce a young child to the world of healthy eating and the importance of trying new foods. The Taste Test activity allows children to explore their senses and develop an appreciation for a variety of foods.

Materials:

- A variety of food items, including fruits, vegetables, and proteins (choose age-appropriate and allergy-friendly options)
- Small plates, bowls, or cups for serving food samples
- Blindfolds (optional)
- Napkins
- Water for cleansing the palate between tastings

Instructions:

1. Begin by discussing the story "The Four Food Fairies" with the children. Talk about the importance of eating various healthy foods and being open to trying new things.

2. Explain to the children that they will be participating in a Taste Test activity, where they will have the opportunity to try small samples of different foods. Encourage them to be open-minded and willing to taste everything offered.

3. Prepare the food samples by cutting the fruits, vegetables, and other items into small, bite-sized pieces. Place each food sample on a small plate, in a bowl, or a cup.

4. Have the children sit at a table or in a circle on the floor. Provide each child with a napkin and a cup of water to cleanse their palate between tastings.

5. If using blindfolds, have the children put them on to heighten their sense of taste (This step is optional, depending on the age and comfort level of the children.)

6. Pass around the food samples one at a time. Encourage the children to describe each item's taste, texture, and smell. Ask questions such as:

- Is the food sweet, salty, sour, or bitter?
- Is the texture smooth, crunchy, or chewy?
- Does the food have a strong or mild smell?

7. After each food sample, have the children cleanse their palates with water before moving on to the next item.

8. When all the food samples have been tasted, remove the blindfolds if used. Discuss the children's favorite and least favorite foods from the taste test.

9. Encourage the children to share their experiences and thoughts about the foods they tried. Discuss the importance of trying new foods and maintaining a balanced diet.

The Taste Test activity encourages children to explore their senses and develop an appreciation for a variety of foods, reinforcing the themes of healthy eating and trying new things found in the story "The Four Food Fairies." By participating in this fun and engaging activity, children can become more open-minded and adventurous in their food choices.

23

The Patchwork Parrot

Embracing diversity, the importance of unity and harmony, empathy and understanding, the power of music, respect for the environment, overcoming challenges

In a lush, enchanting rainforest, where vibrant flowers and overgrown trees created a breathtaking tapestry of color, Patches the Parrot was perched atop a tall tree, marveling at the rich colorings of his feathers. Patches' feathers were unlike ordinary parrots; they formed a beautiful patchwork pattern, each feather a different shade.

One day, as Patches was flying through the rainforest, he noticed that the once-harmonious melodies of the animals had changed. The rainforest creatures were arguing about their differences, believing that their own colors, shapes, and sizes were superior to others. The discord among the animals caused unrest in the rainforest, impacting the lives of others and threatening the delicate balance of the ecosystem. Plants withered as the animals neglected their natural roles, and the once-vibrant rainforest began to lose its luster.

Feeling troubled, Patches decided it was time to remind the rainforest animals about the importance of embracing their differences. He began to visit each group of animals, using his remarkable ability to mimic their sounds and languages. He listened to their stories and shared the wisdom of the patchwork pattern in his feathers.

Patches explained, "Just as each of my feathers has its unique color and pattern, every one of you is special and important in your

own way. Our differences create a beautiful tapestry, and we can create a harmonious melody together."

As Patches spoke to each group, he started to weave a metaphorical musical note out of their stories, representing the essence of their individuality. Once he had collected all the notes, he brought them together to form a radiant rainbow of sound, symbolizing unity and harmony.

With the melody of unity, Patches invited all the animals to gather and celebrate their diversity. As the animals listened to the beautiful song, they began to understand the importance of valuing and appreciating each other's differences.

The animals joined in song, and their voices combined to create a symphony echoing throughout the rainforest. The once harsh notes were now in perfect harmony, and the animals realized their unique traits and backgrounds made their community vibrant and strong. As the animals embraced their differences, the rainforest flourished again, with the plants regaining their vibrant colors and the ecosystem returning to its natural balance.

From that day forward, the rainforest's animals lived in harmony, celebrating their differences and recognizing the beauty in their unique tapestry of colors, shapes, and sizes. And Patches the Parrot, with his wisdom and empathy, continued to spread the message of unity and the importance of embracing diversity, ensuring that the melody of unity would resonate in the hearts of all the creatures in the magical rainforest.

Lessons Revealed

Healing metaphor: The Patchwork Parrot represents the beauty and strength of diversity, with his unique patchwork pattern of feathers symbolizing the importance of accepting and embracing differences. Patches' ability to bring the animals together through the melody of unity serves as a metaphor for harmony and understanding that can be achieved when individuals appreciate each other's uniqueness and work together.

Embracing diversity: Patches the Parrot, with his unique patchwork feathers, serves as a symbol of the beauty found in diversity. The story teaches children to appreciate the differences in others and to understand that these differences make our world more colorful and interesting.

The importance of unity and harmony: The discord among the rainforest animals illustrates the negative effects of failing to appreciate and accept each other's differences. The story shows how restoring unity and harmony allows the rainforest to flourish again, highlighting the importance of living in peace with others.

Empathy and understanding: Patches listens to the stories of the various rainforest animals, demonstrating empathy and understanding. This lesson encourages children to develop these essential skills, allowing them to better connect with others and appreciate their unique perspectives.

The power of music: The melody of unity created by Patches brings the rainforest animals together, symbolizing the power of music to transcend differences and foster a sense of belonging. The story teaches children the importance of using art and creativity to promote understanding and unity.

Respect for the environment: As the animals in the rainforest learn to live in harmony, the ecosystem returns to its natural balance, emphasizing the importance of respecting and caring for the environment. This lesson encourages children to be mindful of their actions and to consider how they may impact the world around them.

Overcoming challenges: Patches takes it upon himself to bring harmony back to the rainforest, demonstrating the importance of taking action to overcome challenges and make a positive impact.

This lesson teaches children the value of perseverance and determination when faced with obstacles.

Suggested Activities

Story retelling: Encourage children to retell the story of The Patchwork Parrot in their own words or through drawings, emphasizing the importance of valuing and appreciating diversity.

Build your own patchwork animal: Provide art materials for children to create their own patchwork animal, complete with unique colors and patterns. Encourage them to share the story behind their animal's diverse appearance.

Diversity discussion: Facilitate a group discussion about the importance of embracing diversity and accepting others' differences. Encourage children to share examples of diversity in their own lives and discuss ways they can celebrate these differences.

Musical melodies: Have children work together to create a musical melody using various instruments or their voices. Emphasize the importance of each individual's contribution to the harmony of the overall piece.

Patchwork art: Have children create a collaborative patchwork art piece using various materials, colors, and textures. Display the finished work as a reminder of the beauty of diversity and unity.

"I Am Unique" activity: Encourage children to create a self-portrait or write a description of their unique characteristics, qualities, and talents. Share these with the group and discuss the importance of valuing individuality.

Read aloud: Read other stories or books that focus on the themes of diversity, acceptance, and unity.

Creative writing: Encourage children to write their own story about a character who learns to appreciate and embrace diversity.

Role-playing: Organize role-playing activities where children can explore different perspectives and learn to understand and empathize with others.

Acts of kindness: Challenge children to perform acts of kindness for others, celebrating and embracing their differences.

"Create Your Own Patchwork Animal" Activity

The Create Your Own Patchwork Animal activity allows children to explore their creativity and celebrate uniqueness by creating their own one-of-a-kind patchwork animals.

Materials:

- Construction paper or card stock in various colors
- Scissors
- Glue or glue sticks
- Markers, colored pencils, or crayons
- Googly eyes (optional)
- Pompoms, sequins, or other embellishments (optional)
- Animal templates (optional)

Instructions:

1. Begin by discussing the story "The Patchwork Parrot" with the children. Talk about the importance of embracing our uniqueness and the beauty of diversity.

2. Explain to the children that they will be creating their own patchwork animals using different colored pieces of paper to represent each animal's unique and diverse qualities.

3. Provide each child with various construction paper or card stock in different colors. Encourage them to select their favorite colors or those representing their unique personalities.

4. Cut out the animal shape. Have the children draw or trace an outline of their chosen animal on one piece of paper. They can use animal templates or draw freehand.

5. Instruct the children to cut various shapes and sizes of "patches" from the other pieces of colored paper. These can be squares, triangles, circles, or any other shape they desire.

6. Have the children glue the patches onto their animal, covering the entire surface with a patchwork pattern. They can overlap the patches to create a layered effect or place them side by side.

7. Once the patchwork pattern is complete, children can use markers, colored pencils, or crayons to add details to their animals, such as eyes, beaks, or whiskers. Alternatively, they can use googly eyes or other embellishments to add character to their creations.

8. Allow the glue to dry completely before displaying the patchwork animals.

9. Encourage the children to share their creations with the group and discuss the unique aspects of each patchwork animal. Talk about how each animal represents the beauty of diversity and the importance of accepting and celebrating our differences.

The Create Your Own Patchwork Animal activity promotes creativity, self-expression, and an appreciation for diversity, reinforcing the themes of the story "The Patchwork Parrot." Children learn to embrace and celebrate their differences by creating unique patchwork animals, just like the patchwork parrot in the story.

24

The Path of Healing Colors

Coping with grief and loss, loss of a family member, understanding and processing emotions, the importance of seeking support, empathy and compassion, resilience and strength, the power of hope

The vibrant forest was home to many creatures, but none were as wise and gentle as Endura the elephant. Endura was known throughout the forest for her ability to help others heal from grief and loss. Her name symbolized strength and perseverance in the face of life's challenges.

One warm, sunny day, a young rabbit named Remy approached Endura with tears glistening in his eyes. He had recently lost his grandfather, and his heart was heavy with sorrow. Having heard of Endura's wisdom, Remy sought her guidance in finding a way to mend his broken heart.

Endura listened to Remy's story and offered to take him along the Path of Healing Colors. She explained that this magical path was a place to explore and understand his feelings, eventually finding comfort and healing through a series of emotional landscapes.

The Path of Healing Colors was divided into different realms, each representing an emotion associated with grief: Sadness, Anger, Longing, Forgiveness, and Hope. As they ventured together, Endura shared her wisdom and taught Remy valuable lessons about processing his emotions and coping with loss.

Their journey began in the Realm of Sadness, a world of soft blues and gentle rain. Endura encouraged Remy to express his

sorrow openly, explaining that tears were like raindrops, washing away the pain and making room for new growth.

As they moved to the Realm of Anger, the landscape shifted to bold reds and fiery oranges. Remy felt a surge of frustration and resentment, but Endura guided him through these feelings, teaching him that anger was a natural part of grieving and that facing it would help him heal.

In the Realm of Longing, the world was awash in shades of purple and twilight. Remy found himself lost in the memories of his grandfather and wished for more time together. Endura gently reminded him that it was essential to cherish the moments they shared while embracing the present.

Upon entering the Realm of Forgiveness, a calm, soothing green landscape unfolded. Endura explained the importance of forgiving oneself and others for unresolved feelings or regrets. As Remy embraced forgiveness, a weight lifted from his heart.

Finally, they reached the Realm of Hope, where the world sparkled with golden light. Endura told Remy that hope was the promise of a brighter future, and while he would always miss his grandfather, he could find comfort in the memories they shared.

Throughout their journey, Endura shared her own experiences of loss, and Remy began feeling a sense of connection and understanding. He realized that he was not alone, and with Endura's guidance, he could learn to navigate his emotions and find healing.

As their journey ended, Remy and Endura returned to the enchanted forest, their hearts lighter and hopeful. Remy thanked Endura for her kindness and wisdom, vowing to share his lessons with others facing grief and loss.

The wise and compassionate elephant, Endura, continued to guide those in need, her name forever symbolizing that strength, resilience, self-compassion, and love can carry us through life's most challenging moments.

Lessons Revealed

Healing metaphor: The Path of Healing Colors represents the emotional journey one takes while processing grief and finding healing. Each realm along the path symbolizes different emotions associated with grief. The changing landscapes and colors embody the various stages of grief and provide a visual representation of the emotional process that occurs during healing.

Understanding and processing emotions: The story takes readers on a journey through the different realms of emotion associated with grief. This encourages children to understand and process their feelings when they experience loss, helping them to heal and grow emotionally.

The importance of seeking support: Remy's decision to seek Endura's guidance demonstrates the importance of reaching out for help during difficult times. This lesson teaches children to seek support from trusted friends or mentors when they are struggling with their emotions.

Empathy and compassion: Endura listens compassionately to Remy's story, showing empathy for his grief and offering guidance on his healing journey. This encourages children to develop empathy and compassion for others who may be experiencing pain or loss.

Resilience and strength: The story emphasizes the importance of resilience and strength in the face of life's challenges. Remy's journey along the Path of Healing Colors teaches him to navigate his emotions and find healing, demonstrating the power of perseverance and determination.

Sharing lessons with others: At the end of the story, Remy vows to share his lessons with others facing grief and loss. This teaches children the value of helping others and using their experiences to support those in need.

The power of hope: The story concludes with Remy and Endura entering the Realm of Hope, emphasizing the importance of maintaining hope during difficult times. This lesson encourages children to remain optimistic and focus on the love and memories they share with those they have lost.

Suggested Activities

Story retelling: Encourage children to retell the story of The Path of Healing Colors in their own words or through drawings, emphasizing the importance of understanding and expressing emotions related to grief and loss.

Create your own emotional landscape: Provide art materials for children to create their own emotional landscapes, reflecting their feelings associated with each realm in the story. Encourage them to share their creations and discuss their experiences with grief, loss, or other challenging emotions.

Grief and loss discussion: Facilitate a group discussion about grief, loss, and the emotions experienced during these challenging times. Encourage children to share their own stories and strategies for coping and healing.

Memory boxes: Have children create a memory box to honor a loved one they have lost or to celebrate a significant life event. Encourage them to fill the box with items that represent their memories, such as photographs, letters, or small keepsakes.

Emotional expression through art: Encourage children to use art to express and explore their emotions. Provide various art materials and encourage them to create pieces that represent their feelings, whether related to grief and loss or other emotional experiences.

Read aloud: Read other stories or books that focus on grief, loss, healing, and emotional expression.

Creative Writing: Encourage children to write their own story about a character who learns to cope with grief and loss.

Role-playing: Organize role-playing activities where children can explore different perspectives and learn to understand and empathize with others experiencing grief and loss.

Mindfulness and meditation: Introduce children to mindfulness and meditation practices that can help them cope with challenging emotions and find healing.

Acts of kindness: Challenge children to perform acts of kindness for others experiencing grief and loss, helping to provide comfort and support.

"Your Emotional Landscape" Activity

In the story "The Path of Healing Colors," Endura takes Remy on a journey through various realms, each representing a different emotion associated with grief. The Create Your Own Emotional Landscape activity allows children to explore their emotions and feelings by creating their own emotional landscapes using colors, shapes, and symbols.

Materials:

- White paper or canvas (at least 11x14 inches)
- Colored pencils, markers, crayons, or watercolor paints
- Paintbrushes and water (if using watercolor paints)
- Optional: magazines or printed images, scissors, glue

Instructions:

1. Begin by discussing the story "The Path of Healing Colors" with the children. Talk about the different emotional realms that

Endura and Remy visit and the colors and symbols associated with each emotion.

2. Explain to the children that they will be creating their own emotional landscapes to represent their feelings using colors, shapes, and symbols.

3. Provide each child with a piece of paper or canvas and their choice of colored pencils, markers, crayons, or watercolor paints.

4. Encourage the children to think about their own emotions and feelings and how they can represent them using colors and shapes. For example, they might use blue for sadness, red for anger, or green for calmness.

5. Have the children create their emotional landscapes by drawing, painting, or collaging different colors, shapes, and symbols onto their paper or canvas. They can create separate sections for different emotions or blend them more abstractly.

6. Children who choose to use magazines or printed images can cut out pictures, patterns, or colors that represent their emotions and glue them onto their paper or canvas.

7. Once the children have completed their emotional landscapes, allow them to share their creations with the group if they feel comfortable doing so. Encourage them to discuss the colors, shapes, and symbols they chose and how they represent their emotions and feelings.

8. Display the emotional landscapes in a designated area, allowing the children to view and appreciate each other's creations.

The Create Your Own Emotional Landscape activity encourages children to explore and express their emotions creatively and visually. By creating their emotional landscapes, children can better understand their feelings and learn how to express and cope with their emotions in a healthy manner.

25

The Garden of Memories

Coping with grief and loss, loss of a pet, the importance of cherishing memories, healing through remembrance, the power of love and friendship, resilience and emotional growth

In the heart of the bustling city, an aging cat named Armani had made his final home. He spent his days watching the hustle and bustle of city life from his cozy apartment window, reflecting on a life filled with love and adventure.

Armani was loved by everyone, especially by a boy named Britt. Britt and Armani shared a special bond and spent countless hours together, exploring the world, listening to the songs of the birds, and watching the sun set behind the hills.

One day, as autumn approached and the leaves began to change colors, Armani felt the cold winds of age tugging at his fur. He knew his time was drawing near, so he shared a secret with Britt. They ventured deep into their favorite park, where Armani showed him a mysterious and magical garden.

In this garden, flowers bloomed in colors that Britt had never seen, and the air filled with the sweetest fragrance. Armani explained that this was the Garden of Memories, where the love and experiences shared between friends could grow into beautiful blossoms that would never fade.

As the days grew shorter, Armani's health began to decline. Britt stayed by his side, sharing stories and laughter and cherishing every moment together. In the blink of an eye, winter arrived, and one snowy morning, Armani's heart grew still.

Everyone mourned the loss of this beloved cat, but none felt the pain as deeply as Britt. His world had turned dark and cold like the winter landscape outside his window.

As Britt lay in his room one day, a delicate snowflake drifted through his window and landed gently on his cheek. The snowflake seemed to whisper, "Remember the Garden of Memories."

Bundling up in his warmest clothes, Britt set out for the park. The snow was deep, but he was determined to reach the magical garden. As he entered the park, he spotted the familiar blossoms in the distance, glowing like a beacon amid the white and barren world.

He felt a warm and gentle breeze when he entered the Garden of Memories. As he walked among the flowers, each seemed to sing a different melody of the memories he had shared with Armani. The laughter and love they had shared bloomed brightly in every petal, chasing away the darkness that had settled in his heart.

As Britt spent time in the garden, he began to understand this place of healing. He realized that even though Armani was no longer with him, their love would continue to bloom in his heart. Like the flowers blossoming from the love he shared with Armani, he could grow and heal from his grief.

Britt's heart grew lighter with each visit to the Garden of Memories, and the flowers around him seemed to grow more vibrant. The warmth and love they shared would never fade away but continue to live on, symbolizing the bond between a boy and his beloved cat.

And so, as the seasons changed and life continued, Britt found solace in the garden, remembering the love and friendship he had shared with Armani. The Garden of Memories became a place of healing and hope, a reminder that love transcends time and that the bonds we share with those we love can never be broken.

Lessons Revealed

Healing metaphor: The Garden of Memories represents the healing power of memories and the enduring love between friends or loved ones, even after they have passed away. The vibrant flowers in the garden symbolize the experiences, emotions, and love shared between Britt and Armani, which continue to blossom and provide comfort to Britt in his time of grief.

Coping with grief and loss: The story follows Britt as he deals with losing his beloved cat, Armani. By sharing his journey through the magical Garden of Memories, the story helps children understand the emotions associated with grief and loss and teaches them how to cope with these feelings.

The importance of cherishing memories: The Garden of Memories is a place where the love and experiences shared between friends can grow into beautiful blossoms that never fade. This lesson encourages children to cherish the memories they create with their loved ones and appreciate their time together.

Healing through remembrance: As Britt visits the garden and remembers the love and friendship he shared with Armani, he finds healing and solace. The story teaches children that remembering their loved ones and shared moments can help them heal and find peace after a loss.

The power of love and friendship: The story emphasizes the unbreakable bond between Britt and Armani, demonstrating the power of love and friendship. This lesson teaches children the importance of forming strong connections with others and cherishing the time they spend with their loved ones.

Resilience and emotional growth: The Garden of Memories helps Britt grow and heal from his grief, teaching him that love transcends time and that the bonds we share with those we love can never be broken. This lesson encourages children to develop resilience and emotional growth, preparing them to face life's challenges with strength and grace.

Suggested Activities

Story retelling: Encourage children to retell the story of The Garden of Memories in their own words or through drawings. This can help them better understand and relate to the themes of love, friendship, loss, and healing.

Create your own Memory Garden: Provide art materials for children to create their own memory gardens, filled with flowers representing the love and memories they have shared with loved ones or pets who have passed away. Encourage them to share their creations and discuss the significance of each flower.

Grief and loss discussion: Facilitate a group discussion about grief, loss, and the emotions experienced during these challenging times. Encourage children to share their own stories and strategies for coping and healing.

Memory jars: Have children create a memory jar to honor a loved one or pet they have lost. Encourage them to fill the jar with items representing their memories, such as photographs, letters, or small keepsakes.

Emotional expression through art: Encourage children to use art to express their emotions. Provide various art materials and encourage them to create pieces that represent their feelings, whether related to grief and loss or other emotional experiences.

Read aloud: Read other stories or books that focus on the themes of love, friendship, loss, and healing.

Creative writing: Encourage children to write their own story about a character who finds comfort and healing in a magical garden after losing a loved one or pet.

Role-playing: Organize role-playing activities where children can explore different perspectives and learn to understand and empathize with others experiencing grief and loss.

Mindfulness and meditation: Introduce children to mindfulness and meditation practices that can help them cope with challenging emotions and find healing.

Acts of kindness: Challenge children to perform acts of kindness for others experiencing grief and loss, helping to provide comfort and support.

"Create Your Own Memory Garden" Activity

In the story "The Garden of Memories," Armani the cat shows Britt a magical garden where memories grow into beautiful, everlasting flowers. The Create Your Own Memory Garden activity allows children to design their own memory gardens, celebrating their cherished memories with loved ones.

Materials:

- White paper or cardboard (at least 11x14 inches)
- Colored pencils, markers, crayons, or watercolor paints
- Paintbrushes and water (if using watercolor paints)
- Optional: magazines or printed images, scissors, glue

Instructions:

1. Begin by discussing the story "The Garden of Memories" with the children. Talk about the magical garden where memories are represented as beautiful flowers and how it helped Britt heal and remember his beloved cat, Armani.

2. Explain to the children that they will be creating their own memory gardens to celebrate and honor their cherished memories with loved ones.

3. Provide each child with a piece of paper and their choice of colored pencils, markers, crayons, or watercolor paints.

4. Have the children think about their own cherished memories and loved ones. Encourage them to consider the colors, shapes, and symbols they associate with those memories.

5. Instruct the children to design their memory gardens by drawing or painting flowers, trees, or other elements representing their memories and loved ones. They can create a unique flower for each memory or design a garden with various elements.

6. If children choose to use magazines or printed images, they can cut out pictures of flowers, trees, or other elements representing their memories and loved ones and glue them onto their paper or cardboard.

7. Once the children have completed their memory gardens, allow them to share their creations with the group if they feel comfortable doing so. Encourage them to discuss the memories and loved ones they chose to include in their gardens.

8. Display the memory gardens in a designated area, allowing the children to view and appreciate each other's creations.

The Create Your Own Memory Garden activity encourages children to celebrate and honor their cherished memories and loved ones. By creating their memory gardens, children can reflect on the importance of remembering and cherishing the moments they've shared with others.

Self-Care for Parents, Teachers, Counselors, and Childcare Providers

Supporting children through their emotional journey can be incredibly rewarding, but it can also be emotionally challenging. Taking care of your own well-being is essential in maintaining the energy, patience, and empathy required to provide support effectively.

Here are some self-care tips to help adults maintain their emotional health while helping children:

Prioritize Self-Care: Schedule a regular time to engage in activities that nourish your mind, body, and soul. This can include exercise, meditation, reading, spending time in nature, or pursuing hobbies you enjoy.

Set Boundaries: Establish and maintain healthy boundaries between your personal and professional life. Ensure you allocate time for rest, relaxation, and connection with friends and family.

Seek Support: Connect with other parents, teachers, or counselors who share similar experiences. Sharing your challenges and successes can provide valuable insights and emotional relief.

Practice Mindfulness: Cultivate a habit of mindfulness through meditation, deep breathing, or journaling to help you stay present, calm, and focused in your interactions with children.

Express Gratitude: Make a conscious effort to focus on your life's and work's positive aspects. Regularly express gratitude for the experiences, relationships, and accomplishments that bring you joy and fulfillment.

Stay Informed: Keep yourself updated with the latest research, tools, and techniques in child psychology and therapy. This can help you feel more confident and effective in your role as a caregiver.

Reflect on Progress: Regularly assess and celebrate the progress you and the children have made together. Recognizing and acknowledging the positive impact of your efforts can be a powerful motivator and an excellent source of emotional resilience.

Be Kind to Yourself: Remember that supporting children through emotional challenges can be tricky, and practicing self-compassion is essential. Acknowledge your efforts and remind yourself that it's okay to have difficult days or moments.

By prioritizing self-care and implementing these strategies, parents, teachers, counselors, and childcare providers can maintain their emotional well-being while providing practical support to children on their healing journey.

About The Author

Harley Sears is an accomplished hypnotherapist with 25 years of experience. His professional journey has included roles as a psychiatric technician for a pediatric hospital, a youth counselor at a home for boys, and a youth mentor for the Army National Guard. Harley earned a Diploma in Hypnotherapy from HMI College of Hypnotherapy in Southern California, a Certificate in Wellness Counseling from Cornell University, and a Specialization in Integrative Health and Medicine from the University of Minnesota. His innovative approach has garnered international attention, enabling him to guide countless individuals toward personal and professional growth. He currently operates a busy private practice in Leawood, Kansas.

Made in the USA
Monee, IL
23 December 2023

49997298R00105